∞

Let There Be
No Divisions Among You

Rev. John MacLaughlin

Let There Be No Divisions Among You

Why All Christians Should Be Catholic

SOPHIA INSTITUTE PRESS

Manchester, New Hampshire

Let There Be No Divisions Among You was formerly published in 1891 by Burns and Oates, London, under the title *Is One Religion as Good as Another?* This 2017 edition by Sophia Institute Press has been abridged and slightly edited to eliminate anachronisms and other anomalies. Where possible, we have identified the persons mentioned by the author as well as the sources of the quotations he cites, leaving untouched the originals where further reliable information was not discoverable.

Printed in the United States of America. All rights reserved.

Cover design by Perceptions Design Studio.

Cover art by Nicole Martin.

Scripture passages in this book are taken from the Douay-Rheims Version of the Bible.

Sophia Institute Press
Box 5284, Manchester, NH 03108
1-800-888-9344

www.SophiaInstitute.com

Sophia Institute Press® is a registered trademark of Sophia Institute.

Library of Congress Cataloging-in-Publication Data

Names: MacLaughlin, John, author.
Title: Let there be no divisions among you : why all Christians should be Catholic / Rev. John MacLaughlin.
Other titles: Is one religion as good as another
Description: Manchester, New Hampshire : Sophia Institute Press, 2017. |
    Originally published under title: Is one religion as good as another? :
    London : Benziger Bros., 1891. | Includes bibliographical references.
Identifiers: LCCN 2016047718 | ISBN 9781622823710 (pbk. : alk. paper)
Subjects: LCSH: Indifferentism (Religion) | Catholic Church—Apologetic works.
Classification: LCC BT33 .M3 2017 | DDC 282—dc23 LC record available at
https://lccn.loc.gov/2016047718

First printing

Contents

Preface vii

Introduction 3

Part 1

There Can Be Only One True Church

1. Reason Disproves Indifferentism 19

2. Revelation Disproves Indifferentism 27

3. The Conversion of Cornelius Refutes Indifferentism . . 39

4. The Council of Jerusalem Rejects Indifferentism 69

5. St. Paul Rejects Indifferentism 81

Part 2

Marks of the One True Church

6. The Criteria 99

7. Unity 103

8. Universality 127

Conclusion 165

Bibliography 175

∞

Preface

It is not without much misgiving that I offer this little book to the public. Were it not that many friends have strongly recommended its publication, I would hardly have the courage to let it appear.

If my tiny effort, however, insignificant though it may be, has no other effect except that of inducing some able and learned ecclesiastic to take up the subject and to deal with it fully and exhaustively, I shall not deem the time I have given to it unprofitably spent.

A portion of the book consists of a development of sermons or lectures delivered — on occasions separated by long intervals — on the points of doctrine that are treated in several of the chapters. The main part of it, however, was written in what I might term "snatches" between missions; and as those missions followed each other in pretty close succession, it was seldom that I had more than a week or a fortnight of consecutive time (rarely even so much) to devote to the work of writing. I have not aimed at style: my chief object has been to bring to the point at issue arguments that might be found solid, clear, conclusive, and convincing.

To prevent its extending beyond the intended limits, I have in the second part, in which I speak of the signs and tokens of truth, treated only two of the marks of the Church—namely, unity and universality. For a similar reason I have not thought it advisable to bring out even these two in all their bearings. I have introduced *only* those features or phases of them that are *necessary* and *sufficient* to distinguish the one true Church from the countless false ones.

The arguments put forward apply to Christians of all denominations who believe in the inspiration of the Scriptures. Some of them may reach the position even of those who, although they do not pretend to take the Bible for their guide, nevertheless profess as much belief in a divine revelation of some kind that saves them from the imputation of utter unbelief or extreme rationalism.

My scope is to show that all religions are not equally right; that one only can be right; that all the rest must be wrong; and, having done this, then to point out the one that *alone* is right among the multitudinous claimants.

What I have written I confidently believe to be trustworthy and in harmony with the constant teaching of the holy Catholic Church; nevertheless, I humbly and unreservedly submit everything contained in the book to the unerring judgment of the same holy Church.

Lastly, while vindicating the truth of the Catholic Faith and while disproving the claims of its antagonists and rivals, I shrink from the idea of saying anything in a tone of sarcasm, or irony, or disrespect; and I utterly disclaim all intention of indulging in personalities of any kind, even by the most distant allusions or insinuations.

John MacLaughlin
Glasgow
Feast of the Most Holy Trinity, June 5, 1887

∞

Let There Be
No Divisions Among You

∞

Introduction

In the following pages I propose to answer the question: "Is one religion as good as another?" In other words, I propose to discuss indifferentism, the popular theory that teaches that all Christian creeds find equal favor in the eyes of God and that it does not matter which branch of Christianity a man belongs to, provided he be a good man after his own fashion.

Now, if we look from a religious standpoint at the elements or sections that constitute the present population of England, leaving for the moment the Roman Catholic community out of sight, we can easily realize that indifferentism is no small problem.

It is true that in one section — which includes several non-Catholic denominations — are found strict, earnest, generous, charitable Protestants, who adhere firmly to the form of religion they have inherited by family tradition and would deem it a violation of conscience to change it for any other; who regard the blessings of Christianity as the greatest good God can bestow upon a people; who contribute liberally to have those blessings spread among the heathen; who advocate Christian education; who bring up their children according to their ideas of strict social morality; who frequent the church, read the Bible, say their prayers, encourage devotion in others, and even make vigorous efforts from time to time to increase the number of their coreligionists by winning proselytes from other denominations.

In another section, however, we find advanced thinkers, agnostics, infidels, and atheists. Whatever name they are to be called by, they no longer believe, or at least profess no longer to believe, in Christianity. They seem to have been borne away into the region of utter unbelief. And however reluctant we may be to realize the fact, this spirit of unbelief has struck its roots more deeply in these countries than many among us seem to imagine.

It was stated in 1860, by those who were likely to have the most reliable information on the subject, that more than five million of the population of England professed no religion of any kind. "Thousands upon thousands," said an earnest advocate of the Establishment[1] some time ago, "are living in London to whom the great truths of the Gospel are practically as little known as if the land of their birth were a heathen land and not the great bulwark of Protestant Christianity."[2] The rector of the important parish of St. Clement, Danes, in the Strand—as reported in the *Quarterly Review* of April 1861—said that he detected in his flock a frightful amount of infidelity—infidelity in all its shapes—extending not merely to the denying of the Christian revelation, but even to the grossest and darkest heathenism.

---

[1] As the legally established religion of England, dioceses and parishes in the Church of England received government subsidies, which provided a substantial portion of their income.

[2] "Spiritual Destitution in the Metropolis," *London Quarterly Review* 109 (1861): 225.

Introduction

Another authority added: "There are whole streets within easy walk of Charing Cross and miles and miles in more obscure places, where the people live literally without God in the world. We could name entire quarters in which it seems to be the custom that men and women should live in promiscuous concubinage; where the very shopkeepers make a profession of atheism and encourage their poor customers to do the same."[3] This same authority laments what he calls the well-known fact that there never was a time when the temper of the lower order was less satisfactory than it is now.

Since that time the spirit of unbelief has not been on the wane. It has never been more rampant than it is at present. The number of those who sneer at the gospel and ridicule everything sacred, instead of decreasing, is increasing every day.

Now, these two sections of the population may be looked upon as its two extreme sections. Between them lies another, and a very large one. It consists of those who profess Christianity, but profess a form of it that is vague and variable and, as such, tends to the destruction of divine revelation altogether.

The creed of this intermediate section of the community teaches that all religions are good—that one is practically as good as another, as all are tending toward the same end; that the great thing is to live up to them—to do what they tell us; that God is indifferent about which formula of faith a man follows, provided he be a good man after his own fashion.

Those who take this view of revelation hold that religion is a matter of opinion, choice, taste, or sentiment and that people may exercise their liberty as freely in choosing it as in choosing

---

[3] Ibid., 241.

the food they eat and the clothes they wear. Or, as Cardinal Manning puts it:

> People today assume that religious truth can have no definite outline and that each man must discover and define it for himself. And no matter how definite he may choose to be, only one law is equally binding on us all: no one must be certain. Each one must concede to his neighbor as much certainty as he claims for himself. The objective certainty of truth is gone. The highest rule of certainty to each is the conviction of his own understanding. And this, in the revelation of God, and in that knowledge which is life eternal.[4]

Such is the theory which is the subject of the following pages. And a most important subject it is—one that ought to be looked upon as all important, not merely by Catholics, but also, for reasons already implied, and which we shall presently explain in detail, by strict Protestants as well.

It is the opinion of those who have the best opportunity of knowing, that indifferentism is the chief obstacle to conversion to the Catholic Faith in England. And it is the opinion of the same authorities that it is sending people in large numbers every year from Anglicanism into agnosticism or infidelity. It may not land them there all at once, but it puts them on the road that leads there. Hence, although it is the enemy of the Catholic Church by keeping many out of her communion, it is no less

[4] Cardinal Manning, *The Grounds of Faith*, 5. Henry Edward Manning (1808–1892) was the Roman Catholic archbishop of Westminster, England, from 1865 until his death in 1892. Originally an Anglican cleric, he converted to Catholicism in 1851.

the enemy of the Protestant church by sweeping numbers of her children into the ranks of unbelief. In preventing them from coming to Rome, it does not, on that account, make them hold more firmly to the Anglican formularies—it rather tends to ripen them for utter infidelity.

When I say it is the enemy of the Catholic Church, I do not mean that it is so from bigotry, bitter hostility, or determined opposition, for it is too tolerant of every form of belief to be sternly opposed to any. I mean it is the enemy of the Catholic Church by keeping many out of her fold. This is worth considering. There are many obstacles to England's conversion: chief among them is the spirit of indifferentism, liberalism, latitudinarianism, or whatever name we may call it by. It stands to reason it should be so.

When a man has gone so far as to regard religion as a mere matter of opinion, and consequently as a matter of choice, he is not likely to choose a difficult one when an easy one will suit his purpose quite as well. Naturally, men are averse to having their intellect bound to definite doctrines and to having their will burdened by difficult obligations.

There are few, if any, who will think of embracing a creed that imposes many restraints, while they feel, or at least try to feel, that they can go to heaven equally safely by one that imposes hardly any restraint at all. Why should I be asked to waste time in considering the claims of a Church that makes marriage a contract that can never, under any circumstances, be dissolved, and that binds her members to confession and to receive the Eucharist at least once a year, to assist at a certain form of worship every Sunday, to fast at stated times, to abstain on certain days from meat, and to obey spiritual pastors while I am free to remain in, or to join, a church that imposes no obligations of the kind? As long as men are satisfied that all religions are equal in the sight of God, there is little hope of their seeking after any that differs from the easy one to which they have been accustomed.

It is quite different in the case of the strict, earnest, practical Protestant, who becomes uneasy in conscience about the truth of the creed he has hitherto professed. When *he* gets unsettled in his belief and entertains a serious doubt as to its tenableness, he is at once involved in researches; he will inquire, read, pray; he is willing to put himself to inconvenience, and even to make sacrifices, in his anxious search after truth.

But the man who enjoys unruffled peace in the wide and easy creed of indifferentism is not likely to trouble himself with pondering on the claims of a Church that exacts stern, unchanging faith in her doctrines and is constantly enforcing the strict fulfillment of her precepts. Such a man will never look toward Rome except through the influence of some very special grace. And the longer he remains the adherent of a system that is only an excuse for indolence and apathy, the further he drifts away from the definite teaching and strict discipline of the Catholic Church.

Hence, until you have banished entirely from his thoughts the conviction that one religion is as good as another, until you have cleared away from his mind the shifting sands of indifferentism, you will not be able to lay in his understanding a foundation for definite faith. Or, as Cardinal Newman remarks, "You cannot build in the aboriginal forest till you have felled the trees."[5]

But although indifferentism is the enemy of the Church of Rome, it is no less the enemy of the Church of England. It tends

[5]   John Henry Newman, *Lectures on the Present Position of Catholics in England: Addressed to the Brothers of the Oratory,* 2nd ed. (London: Burns and Lambert, 1851), viii.

to destroy her, although it is her offspring. It has sprung from the free application of her great principle of private judgment. And the older it grows, and the larger it becomes, the more seriously does it threaten her life.

Through it, multitudes of her members become an easy prey to infidelity. In fact, we may say, it is a kind of preparatory school for infidelity. When men are hanging only loosely to Christianity by the elastic thread of indifferentism, a very slight influence is sufficient to make them abandon it altogether and leave them without faith in anything beyond the world of sense.

The theory that one religion is as good as another is next neighbor to the theory that there is not much good in any religion at all.

If religion is only an opinion, then every religion may be wrong, since every opinion may be wrong. And as every religion may be wrong, there is no possibility of ever arriving at any certainty about those matters that religion professes to deal with: the whole thing from that moment becomes lost in impenetrable darkness. The mysteries of faith are then denied because they appear opposed to reason; and when the mysteries of faith are set aside, Christianity as a revelation of new and definite doctrines disappears. This state of mind gradually prepares a man for the wholesale denial of Christianity as a divine revelation; and hence the step from indifferentism into utter unbelief is natural and easy.

But let us come from the abstract to the concrete, from possibilities to things that are taking place in actual life under our own eyes. See what is going on in our midst. It is no secret that the rapid growth of unbelief, chiefly among persons of education, is due mainly to the fact that the ceaseless divisions in the various branches of Anglicanism have generated in the minds of many the conviction that Christianity is a failure. Numbers of men, formerly Protestants, and, for the most part, men of cultivated intellect, have declared that they have ceased to believe in Christian revelation altogether, in consequence of the Church of England tolerating within her pale absolutely contradictory teaching on the most fundamental doctrines of the Christian creed. Such men could never reconcile themselves to the view that that church was, as she professed to be, a divine teacher when she approved totally opposite views of the religion of which she was the recognized organ.

Now, when people of non-Catholic denominations thus lose all confidence in the religion they have hitherto professed, they do not, as a rule, look, or care to look, in any other direction for consistency and truth. They find no book, or at all events they read no book, that would have the effect of turning their thoughts toward that one sanctuary of truth, that everlasting treasure house, in which alone are found harmonious unity, unchanging doctrine, perfect consistency, everything that can satisfy the cravings of the human mind—that is, the Catholic Church.

On the other hand, the infidel literature of the day, which is pouring from the press like a deluge and which threatens to submerge the greater part of the earth, easily finds its way into their hands. It preaches a new gospel—one just suited to their present temper of mind; it pronounces Christianity a myth, a fable, an antiquated superstition, a bundle of conflicting doctrines that cannot bear the test of scientific investigation.

The shallow, blasphemous arguments of the New Gospel are clothed in that elegant sophistry that its ingenious propagandists know so well how to use. These arguments meet with hardly any resistance in the mind of the Christian indifferentist who has no definite form of belief to cling to. He has seen nothing but contradiction in the creed he has been accustomed to, and he is captivated by the apparently more consistent principles of infidelity. He becomes its disciple.

He gives himself up unreservedly to its teaching; and he does so all the more willingly, because, whereas his late Christian profession imposed upon him some semblance of moral restraint, infidelity relieves him of restraint altogether. He is no longer crippled by the pains of conscience. He becomes dead to all sense of moral responsibility. He can go where inclination leads and give loose reins to his passions and gratify every desire with impunity; for while he hopes for no future reward, he fears no future punishment.

Indifferentism, then, liberalism in religion, latitudinarianism, acted on by the infidel press of the day, is sending thousands of members every year from the Establishment into atheism. It is sapping her very foundations. Hence, to say the least, Protestants have as much reason to hate it as Catholics have.

The injury it inflicts on Protestantism is greater than the injury it inflicts on Catholicism. The one is negative, the other positive. Whereas it tends only to put further and further away from the Church of Rome people who never belonged to her, and renders them less disposed to examine her claims, on the other hand, it robs the Establishment of multitudes of her baptized members and consigns them to hopeless unbelief. This it has been doing; this it is doing still; this it will continue to do. And the end will be, says a writer of this generation, that it will sweep so many from her ranks into the region of the "unknowable" that whenever the state withdraws its sustaining hand, as soon as those props and buttresses by which the civil power keeps her standing give way, she will totter and fall to pieces; and in the day of her downfall there will be few sincere adherents remaining to weep over her dissolution.

Bossuet foresaw this and predicted it. Speaking of the great revolt of the sixteenth century, and referring specially to England, he says:

Every man erects a tribunal for himself where he becomes the arbiter of his own belief. Although the innovators wished to restrain the minds of men within the limits of Holy Scripture, yet as each individual was constituted its interpreter and was to believe that the Holy Scripture would discover to him its meaning, all were authorized to worship their own inventions, to consecrate their own errors, and to place the seal of the Divinity on their own thoughts. It was then foreseen that by this unbridled license, sects would be multiplied to infinity, and that while some would not cease to dispute or to hold their reveries for inspirations, others, wearied by visions of folly, and not able to recognize the majesty of religion, torn asunder by so many sects, would seek at length a fatal repose and complete independence in indifference to all religion, or Atheism.[6]

Dr. Moriarty,[7] lately bishop of Kerry, who, in his allocution to his clergy on *The Church Establishment*, quotes the above passage, adds:

---

[6] From Jacques-Bénigne Bossuet's November 19, 1669, "Funeral Oration of Henriette-Marie," the widow of Charles I of England. Bossuet (1627–1704) was a French bishop and theologian renowned for his eloquent sermons.

[7] Bishop David Moriarty (1814–1877).

Introduction

Why was not the latter part of this prophecy sooner and more universally fulfilled among us? What was it that retarded the erring mind in its downward path toward infidelity? While Protestantism elsewhere rapidly changed into Rationalism, in these countries it even yet retains a large portion of Christian truth. The material and golden bond of an endowed Establishment furnishes the only reasonable explanation we can suggest for its standing still upon the steep incline. Besides the rewards offered to orthodoxy, its connection with the State preserved while it enslaved it; the dry, hard, unyielding discipline of law and government insisted on the observance of forms and formularies and thus kept Protestantism in shape, as bodies though lifeless are preserved in ice.[8]

Cardinal Newman considers this theory to be the religion of half the population of England. Anyone who has mixed much with the masses and has seen how widely it is spread and the hold it has taken on the mind of the multitude must feel that his estimate is not beyond the mark. The popularity it has attained in all classes of society is astounding. It may be justly named the most popular creed of the day.

In mixing with people of non-Catholic denominations in the large towns and country districts of England, I have frequently asked persons who were not Catholics (but whose Catholic connections desired me to put the question) whether they had any objection to becoming members of the Roman Catholic communion. On most occasions the answers I received indicated

---

[8] David Moriarty, *A Letter on the Disendowment of the Established Church* (Dublin: John F. Fowler, 1867), 15.

clearly enough that this flexible system of indifferentism was their only creed. They spoke as if they were perfectly satisfied with it and seemed to have no appetite for anything in the shape of religion beyond it.

Repeatedly I have heard candid, straightforward professions such as the following: "I cannot say that I have any objection to the Roman Catholic religion"; "One religion is as good as another"; "All religions are good"; "It makes no matter what we are when we are Christians at all." Avowals such as these made it clear that the persons from whom they came had no idea of the necessity of belonging to any one definite Christian creed or of holding fast to any special doctrine of revelation.

They spoke as if they might choose a religion today and change it tomorrow, and change the one of tomorrow for a directly opposite one the day following, and repeat these changes until they had gone around the whole circle of Christian sects; and as if they might do all this without imperiling their salvation in any way whatever, at least as far as forms of belief were concerned.

While I mean this little book chiefly for persons such as these who are outside the Church, I mean it also for some who are within. There are Catholics who are disposed to make concessions that their Church can never warrant. They move in a circle of society or are placed in circumstances where they are strongly tempted to temporize in matters of religion. They may be inclined to attach much more importance to expediency, or to certain false notions of etiquette, than to duty even of a sacred kind. For example, they hear it stated in some drawing-room assembly, or at some nobleman's dining table, where the tone of the conversation is notably Protestant, that, after all, one religion is quite as good as another — that there is hardly any difference of any importance, that it is quite immaterial what creed a man follows, provided he be an honest man, pay twenty shillings in the pound, do no injury to his neighbor in his property or in his character, and discharge his duty faithfully as a benevolent member of society.

Now, if they (Catholics) chime in with this liberal doctrine, endorse it, express assent to it, or imply assent to it, they are simply encouraging heresy, virtually propagating it, sacrificing their most sacred convictions to erroneous ideas of politeness or rather, allowing themselves to be swayed by the lowest and most despicable form of human respect. They imagine, perhaps, that by this kind of liberalistic spirit they will find favor in the eyes of those who are above them in social position. It is just the contrary. Even the very persons whose esteem they wish to gain or to retain in making admissions that their Church and their own conscience condemn will soon begin to look on them with contempt and distrust. The Catholic Church cannot tolerate any compromise. She is not at liberty to allow even the least morsel of error to be mixed up with the sacred deposit of truth that has been entrusted to her.

And hence she can never countenance the low, groveling complaisance of those who seek to further their own interests by expressing their approbation of statements that are entirely at variance with her teachings. Of course, I do not mean that the Catholic faithful ought to be eager to engage in controversy, to be uselessly parading their Faith, or to be obtruding it in an offensive manner upon others. But I do mean that it is altogether unlawful for them to sanction, either explicitly or implicitly, a system of religion that embodies the subtlest, popular, and dangerous heresy of the present day — that broad and wide Christianity that teaches that all religions find equal favor in the eyes of God. "In private life," says Cardinal Manning, "we ought to be kindly and unobtrusive, but uncompromising in confessing our Faith; never forcing it upon the unwilling, but never silent when we ought to speak."[9]

---

[9] Cardinal Manning, "Sermon on Indifference," Advent, 1884.

Part 1

∞

There Can Be Only
One True Church

Chapter 1

∞

Reason Disproves Indifferentism

One of the most popular, plausible, and at the same time pernicious theories about religion today is the theory that teaches
that a man may be quite indifferent to what Christian creed he
belongs, provided he be a good man after his own fashion. This
theory may be called by some latitudinarianism, by others liberalism in religion, by others indifferentism. Whatever name we
give it, it means simply the doctrine that one religion is as good
as another, or that all creeds are equally agreeable in the eyes of
God. Its advocates say, and say in the plainest terms, that God
does not care what religion His creatures profess, provided they
live up to and act consistently with the one they have embraced
or the one that has been handed down to them by family tradition. They contend, in fact, that men may claim as large a measure of liberty in choosing the creed they profess as in choosing
their place of residence or their family doctor. Instead of making
religious belief a matter of duty, they, on the contrary, make it
a matter of choice, taste, sentiment, and inclination. They act
and speak and think, or at least affect to think, that while God
holds up, as it were, before men's minds certain doctrines that He
commands to be believed, men are, nevertheless, free to put aside

those doctrines and to choose other doctrines, *even contradictory ones*, in their stead.

Their reasoning, when analyzed, must force them inevitably to the conclusion that although the voice of the God of everlasting truth has declared something to be true, they are at liberty to believe it to be false; and that while that same unerring voice proclaims some statement to be false, they, in the enjoyment of the fullness of their right of private judgment, are free to look upon it as true. Liberty of choice with regard to forms of Christian belief means nothing less than this.

Does this theory, which eloquent sophistry has made so plausible, deserve the popularity that it has attained and that has given it such a hold on the mind of the multitude?

No. So far from deserving the approbation, it does not deserve even the toleration of any reasonable man. Let us weigh it in the balance of truth. Let us look at it in the light of right reason and of divine revelation, and we shall find that it contradicts at once man's reason and God's revelation.

First, we shall deal with it as a contradiction of reason.

God being what He is, that is, the God of eternal truth, He cannot be indifferent as to whether His people believe this particular creed or some other creed that contradicts it. To say that He does not care what form of Christianity they profess is exactly equivalent to saying that He does not care whether they believe what is true or what is false. For the different creeds that now exist, and that press their claims on the homage of man's mind, contradict each other — and not merely in small items of belief, but even in doctrines that are commonly looked upon as fundamental by those belonging to any Christian denomination.

One Church teaches that Christ is truly, really, and substantially present in the sacrament of the Eucharist; another church teaches that He is not truly present in the sacrament of the Eucharist. One Church teaches that the priest has power to forgive the grievous sins committed after Baptism; another church teaches that the priest has not power to forgive the grievous sins committed after Baptism. One Church holds that the pope has universal spiritual jurisdiction over the whole world and that his utterances are infallible when he speaks on faith and morals in certain given circumstances; other churches maintain that the pope has not universal spiritual jurisdiction over the whole world and that his utterances are not infallible in those circumstances in which members of the Roman Catholic communion say they are infallible.

Now, here are statements, and here are contradictory statements—contradictory statements in matters of great moment—in doctrines that touch even the very foundations of faith. The voice of reason is peremptory and emphatic. It proclaims, in a tone that cannot be mistaken, that the creed that affirms these propositions and the creed that denies them cannot be both true. Two statements that contradict each other cannot both be true at once. Only one can be true; the other must be false; and the evident truth of one establishes the evident falsehood of the other.

To say, therefore, that God does not care whether His people profess this religion or that other religion that is in contradictory opposition to it, is exactly the same as to say that He does not care whether they believe truth or falsehood.

Now, philosophy (which is a science of reason) demonstrates that veracity, or essential truthfulness, is one of God's attributes. In virtue of this essential attribute, God not only loves truth but necessarily loves truth; and He not only hates falsehood but must, as a law of His being, bear an undying, eternal hatred toward it. And hence, to affirm that He leaves people free to believe what is true or what is false, as they choose, is nothing short of a blasphemy against His attribute of essential truthfulness.

The moment we affirm that one religion is as good as another, and that it is a matter of indifference with God as to what form of Christian belief men adopt, that moment we are hurried inevitably into the blasphemous conclusion that He is not more glorified by the profession of the doctrines that He Himself has revealed than He is by the profession of those false theories of men that contradict them. If *He* has condescended to reveal from on high one definite religion (and all professing Christians freely admit that He has done so), surely He cannot be indifferent about whether that one definite religion that He has thus revealed or some other religion that is in open, palpable opposition to it is believed.

This statement, which is clear enough in its bare enunciation, will become still clearer in the light of the following illustrations. We read in the Old Testament that when the Israelites, in their journey through the desert, had reached the wilderness of Sinai, having the mountain of Sinai over against them, the time had come when God was to make known the Ten Commandments, and to have a tabernacle and an ark constructed for His worship. It was on that memorable occasion that He revealed to Moses the precise plan according to which both tabernacle and ark were to be made. He was not content with describing the general dimensions, such as the length, the breadth, and the height; He went down to the minutest details. He specified the particular kind of wood of which both were to be made, i.e., setim wood.[10] He specified also the particular way in which they were to be

[10] Or acacia wood. See Exod. 25:10ff.

overlaid with gold; and He added the other precious materials that were to be used in their decoration.

No human architect could enter more minutely into details, in giving a design for some earthly structure, than the great Divine Architect did on that occasion, when there was question of giving the plan after which His ark and tabernacle were to be fashioned. And if He was so explicit in the directions He gave, it was simply because He meant to show that He would not leave any room for the promptings of man's imagination, fancy, or private judgment in the construction of those sacred appurtenances for His worship.

Hence, He charged Moses, in words on which He laid all the emphasis His divine voice could command, to keep to and not to depart in the least item from the plan that had been revealed to him. "Look," He said, "and make it [the ark] according to the pattern which was shown thee in the mount."[11]

Now let us suppose that as soon as Moses had gone down from the mountain, he had begun to make the tabernacle and the ark, not according to the plan that had been divinely revealed to him, but according to a plan struck out of his own head. Would God have sanctioned the change? If Moses had departed from the pattern thus divinely shown to him, and shown to him in such minute, precise, definite detail, and had constructed tabernacle and ark according to the dictates of his own private judgment, God would not have recognized either as the thing that He had commanded to be made.

And surely we cannot say that the God of infinite knowledge, of infinite wisdom, of eternal truth, is more concerned about the length and breadth of a material thing than about

---

[11] Cf. Exod. 25:40.

those momentous truths that go to build up the noble, majestic structure of His religion.

The conversation between Moses and God on the mountain furnishes us with another illustration that is quite as much to the point. It directs our thoughts in the same channel. It was there that God gave him, written with His own finger on tables of stone, those Ten Commandments that were to form the basis of all moral law. He directed Him to make these Commandments known to the people. Such was the commission given to Moses, and such the message he was to announce. His work was marked out for him. He was not the maker of the law; he was but the vehicle by which it was to pass to the people. When he received those binding precepts from the hands of that great sovereign Lord and Creator, to whom man owed both the homage of the mind and the service of the body, he was not at liberty to put them aside and give to the people precepts of his own making. He had no power to change the law, of which those precepts were the expression. He could not add to it; he could not take away from it. He was bound to give it to the people as he himself received it, in all its purity, integrity, and definiteness.

On the other hand, similar obligations rested on the people as soon as the promulgation of those precepts reached them. When they heard them from the lips of Moses, who announced them in the name of God, whose representative he was, they were not free to depart from them and to frame for themselves other precepts that would be more in harmony with their natural inclinations. No, there was the divine code — there the expression of God's law for man clear, distinct, definite; and man was bound to follow it and forbidden to follow any that was at variance with it.

Now, Moses appeared in the Old Dispensation as the oracle of Divine Truth to those of whom he was the chief, as the medium of that partial revelation that God then vouchsafed to make to His people.

Jesus Christ appeared in the New Dispensation, when the fullness of time was come, to reveal additional doctrines to the world—doctrines immeasurably more important. And if those who lived in the centuries that intervened between the days of Moses and the Incarnation were obliged to adhere to the portion of revelation made to them through the lips of that great Law-giver, surely the people of the present dispensation are as strictly obliged to embrace and adhere to that religion, when it has been enlarged, completed, and perfected by God's own Incarnate Son, who is the Way, the Truth, and the Life.

The foregoing arguments may be summed up in these two sentences: first, right reason can never sanction contradiction and therefore can never sanction indifferentism; second, if God does not allow any change to be made in the plan He gives for the construction of a material sanctuary for His worship, it is against all reason to hold that He will allow any change to be made in the doctrines that teach in what His true worship con-sists—that is, in the truths He wishes to be believed and the laws He wishes to be fulfilled.

Chapter 2

∞

Revelation Disproves Indifferentism

The theory of indifferentism is also a contradiction of revelation. After His Resurrection from the dead, and before He ascended to His Father, our Divine Lord appeared on a mountain in Galilee. His Apostles were there to meet Him. His appearing on that particular mountain had been expected; it had been previously announced by Him. It was natural that it should be a meeting of special appointment. It was one of unequaled import. Its results were to sway the world to the end of time. The interests of the whole human race would be influenced by it. It was there that our Divine Lord gave to His Apostles that great commission to which the world owes its conversion. "Going," He said to them, "teach ye all nations, baptizing them in the name of the Father, and of the Son, and of the Holy Spirit, teaching them to observe all things whatsoever I have commanded you. And behold I am with you all days, even to the consummation of the world."[12]

"Teach ye all nations," He said. What were they to teach? They were to teach the truths of His Faith and the precepts of

---

[12] Matt. 28:19–20.

His law. And they were to teach all nations these selfsame truths and precepts. He could not mean that, when they divided the earth into those vast districts that were to be the spheres of their respective apostolates, one Apostle was to preach in one country that there was a sacrament in the Church by which the sins committed after Baptism could be forgiven and another Apostle was to preach in another country that there was no such sacrament. Neither could he mean, when He thus sent them forth in His name, that He authorized some among them to announce that He was truly and really and substantially present in the sacrament of the Eucharist and that He authorized others of them to preach the contradictory, i.e., that He was *not* truly present in that sacrament. No, He left no room for the play of fancy or the promptings of imagination or the dictates of private judgment. He would have them understand, and understand beyond all manner of doubt, that as He was the one, only God, so there could be only one true religion that was the faithful expression of His divine mind to His people.

Being the God of essential truthfulness, He would not allow man's error to be mixed up with His truth. He would permit no human authority to add to His doctrines, nor would He permit any human authority to diminish them.

Mark well the words that He added, with such significance and such emphasis, when He gave His Apostles the great world-wide commission to teach. They call for special notice, for we must remember that they were sounded by that same omnipotent voice that spoke to Moses on Sinai when the great commission of promulgating the Ten Commandments was given him, and when the plan of the ark and of the tabernacle was shown him; and when God said to him: "Look and make it after the pattern that was shown thee on the mount."

We must remember, too, that the Apostles and their successors had as little power to change the doctrines they were then commissioned to preach as Moses had to change the Ten Commandments or to change the plan according to which the ark and the tabernacle were to be constructed.

The words in question prove this. "Teaching them," He said, "to observe *all* things whatsoever I have commanded you." He did not say, "Teaching them to observe this portion of what I have commanded you"; nor did He say, "Teaching them to observe that other portion of what I have commanded you"; but He said, "Teaching them to observe *all things whatsoever* I have commanded you." *All things*, whether in the domain of faith or in the domain of morals.

It was as if He had said, "You are not to teach them that they may observe whatever they will take into their heads to observe or whatever their individual preference or private judgment may dictate; nor are you to teach them that they may observe whatever *your* own private judgment dictates or *your* imagination prompts; but you are to teach them to observe all things whatsoever I have commanded you — these things and nothing else. You are to make them feel that they have no liberty of choice, that I will never tolerate the innovations of human opinion upon the doctrines that, through my Church, I teach, or upon the laws that, through her, I enforce."

May we not say that these words — "Teaching them to observe all things whatsoever I have commanded you" — without straining them in the least, without stretching them beyond their natural obvious import, are equivalent to a positive, absolute condemnation of the theory of indifferentism? For did not these words mean something definite and certain in the mind of our Lord? Did He not intend them to mean something definite and certain in the minds of His Apostle? And did He not intend *by* them to empower and oblige His Apostles to convey that definite and certain "something" to the nations that they were to teach?

But the argument gathers additional strength from the fact that when our Lord gave to His Apostles this great worldwide commission to teach, He knew well how much it would cost them to carry it out. The future lay as clear before Him, being God as well as man, as did the past and the present. The stern, desperate opposition they must meet with — the sufferings, the humiliations, the privations they must endure in their long, laborious career, were all present to His mind when He spoke the words, "Going, teach all nations." He saw their scourgings, the prisons in which they would be chained, the days and nights they must pass in hunger, thirst, and cold. He saw, too, the violent deaths that were in store for them. And He saw all these things not in vague outline, but in all their terrible, revolting, and harrowing details. He saw the shipwrecks, the imprisonments, the cauldron of boiling oil, the flaying alive, the beheading, the crucifixion with head downward. He knew well that their lives were to be lives of unceasing toil, pain, and contempt, and that their deaths were to be the deaths of malefactors.

Yet these men were His chosen ones. They were His dearest friends; nearly all of them had been with Him throughout his public life — the men whom He loved with the fondest love of His sacred, loving Heart.

But how to reconcile the love He bore them, and His clear foreknowledge of their lifelong martyrdom, with the statement that He is quite indifferent to which faith people hold, provided they act consistently with it? Would it not have been cruel on His part thus to doom His special servants, His dearest friends, to those lives of suffering and deaths of shame if it was a matter of no consequence to Him whether His people worshipped Him according to this creed or that? If men, by acting consistently with whatever idea of religion they already held, became sufficiently acceptable to Him, why not leave them as they were, and save the Apostles from such trials in life and such torments in death?

Let them act in accordance with the lights of nature — those lights gave them a certain notion of religion; that notion of it, though full of error, was for them as good as any other (according to the principles of our opponents) if their life was in harmony with it.

Or, in case some fragment of definite positive revelation by chance reached them, through conversation with the Jews, or through the promulgation of Christianity at Jerusalem, let them use it according to casual or ordinary helps. And let further illumination, if deemed expedient, for some particularly privileged soul (like the centurion Cornelius[13]) be vouchsafed by the ministry of an angel.

But why condemn an Apostle to a life of incessant pain and a death of unheard-of torment in order to bring to his fellowman a message of salvation if his fellowman was free (in spite of every evidence of its truth) to accept that message or to reject it, or to accept a part and reject the rest, and could make himself quite as agreeable to God without it as with it?

Does not the fact of His giving that great commission to His Apostles prove that He meant them to convey to His people some definite message of revelation which His people could not know by any natural means? And does not His foresight of the

[13] See Acts 10.

storms of persecution they were to encounter and the tremendous trials they were to undergo, show how extremely important He considered it that that message should reach them? Who can give us permission to treat as insignificant or to be indifferent about a message — or the true meaning of a message — to which a God of infinite wisdom attached so much importance? None but He could give such permission, and He could not do so without defeating His own ends.

I can easily anticipate the argument that will spring to the lips of indifferentists in answer to this reasoning. It is in vain, however, for them to urge it. The very comprehensiveness of their system makes it powerless. They say that the Apostles were sent to teach and to preach, in order that men might know and believe in Christ, the Mediator, whose mediation or redemption was the leading idea or the great fundamental truth, of the gospel — a truth that men could not know by the light of reason or by any revelation made heretofore to the Jews.

But the very men who say this comprise in their theory of liberal religion Socinians and Unitarians, who do not believe in the divinity of Christ at all — do not believe in Original Sin — do not believe in Redemption — who reject all the mysteries of religion from the very fact that they *are* mysteries and that, therefore, reason cannot comprehend them.

I mean, they will tell us that the Socinian or Unitarian who acts in accordance with what his religion teaches, can quite as easily find favor in the eyes of God, and therefore quite as easily save his soul as the man who professes the most detailed and most complete form of Christian belief; and that it is a matter of indifference to God whether a man chooses for his creed Unitarianism pure and simple, which absolutely denies the mystery of Redemption, or chooses some other formula of religion that emphatically affirms that mystery as one of the most vital doctrines of Christianity.

The conclusion from such premises is clear. It must be this: it was quite useless to put the Apostles to such trouble, to force them to lead a life of perpetual self-sacrifice in announcing the doctrine of Redemption, since men, although living in a country where that doctrine is widely professed, clearly explained, and sustained by sound and convincing proofs, are free to form and cling to a creed from which it is sedulously excluded. And while exercising such wide liberty in the choice of a creed, they are doing an act that in itself is quite as acceptable in the eyes of God and quite as apt to promote salvation as would be the act of faith made by him whose creed contains with absolute certainty all those doctrines our Lord referred to when He said to His Apostles, "Teaching them to observe all things whatsoever I have commanded you."

But there is another answer to this sophistry. On what grounds does the indifferentist, or the latitudinarian, or the advocate of any form of liberal religion single out the mystery of Redemption or any other isolated doctrine of Christianity, as *the* one for whose promulgation the Apostles *principally* were to traverse the earth, spend their lives in toil, shed their blood, and die a martyr's death?

Were not those Apostles as strictly bound to announce all the doctrines that the Redeemer taught as they were to announce the truth that *He* was the Redeemer? Is not this evident from the words He Himself made use of when He gave them the worldwide commission—"Teaching them to observe all things whatsoever I have commanded you"? Was there anything in that commission, either expressed or understood, to warrant them in believing that He gave them leave to class His doctrines under the heads of principal and subordinate, or to put forward some as of primary and others as of secondary importance? Did they not look upon everything that came from His lips as equally important and equally grave? Did they claim to have any share in formulating the creed they were to teach by choosing some of His precepts and rejecting others? Did they not know that to reject one iota of His revelation was to deny His authority altogether? And did not the same reasons that bound the people who were taught by the Apostles to believe some of the gospel truths bind them to believe *all* the gospel truths?

What reason could there be for receiving part and for rejecting the rest? Why believe the Apostles to be credible up to a certain point and look upon them as totally unworthy of credence beyond that point? But, above all, why should the Apostles be sent to preach at all, if it mattered so little whether men believed or did not believe even those doctrines that are looked upon by most Christians as the leading fundamental doctrines of the gospel? Must not then the preaching of the Apostles (in the theory of our opponents) be regarded as vain and meaningless?

Cardinal Newman, in his book entitled *Discussions and Arguments*, traces the sad issue to which this "marking out" or "singling out" of favorite doctrines leads:

> Many would fain discern one or two doctrines in the Scripture clearly and no more; or some generalized form, yet not so much as a body of doctrine of any character. They consider that a certain message, consisting of one or two great and simple statements, makes up the whole of the Gospel, and that these are plainly in the Scriptures: accordingly, that he who holds and acts upon these is a

Christian, and ought to be acknowledged by all to be such, for in holding these he holds all that is necessary. These statements they sometimes call the essentials, the peculiar doctrines, the leading idea, the vital doctrines, the great truths of the Gospel; and all this sounds very well; but when we come to realize what is abstractedly so plausible, we are met by this insuperable difficulty, that no great number of persons agree together what are those great truths, simple views, leading ideas, or peculiar doctrines of the Gospel. Some say that the doctrine of the Atonement is the leading idea; some the doctrine of spiritual influence; some that both together are the peculiar doctrines; some that love is all in all; some that the acknowledgment that Jesus is the Christ and some that the resurrection from the dead; some that the announcement of the soul's immortality is, after all, the essence of the Gospel, and all that need be believed.[14]

Then, in the words that he subjoins, and which we have already quoted, he shows that the indifferentist, following out his principles of latitude, may, without any inconsistency, deny even the dogma of the Trinity; and that if that great fundamental mystery is put aside, mystery gradually disappears from the Christian creed altogether. He observes also that the gospel under the destructive influence of indifferentism becomes merely an equivalent for a new publication of the law of Nature. In other words, the indifferentist, who believes himself a Christian because he professes this broad, undefined Christianity, is

[14] John Henry Newman, *Discussions and Arguments on Various Subjects*, 3rd ed. (London: Pickering, 1878), 127–128.

pretty much on a level with those who are entirely outside the pale of Christendom, whom no ray of revealed religion has ever reached — that is, as far as divine faith is concerned, he is on a level with such. As to salvation, it may be said that his chances of being saved are less, since he rejects lights that were never offered to the heathen — unless, indeed, he be one of those in whose case good faith or invincible ignorance may plead in their behalf.

The inevitable results to which latitudinarianism, indifferentism, and liberalism in religion leads could not be more beautifully or more accurately described than in the words of the great cardinal that I have quoted, which were written by him several years before he became a Catholic.

To hold that every man's view of revealed religion is acceptable to God if he acts in accordance with it, that no one view is in itself better than another, is simply to reduce Christianity to a level with morality — to lead men on gradually, although it may be slowly, to the gulf of absolute unbelief.

Now, if a theory, whose natural tendency is to lead to such lamentable consequences, is maintainable, then the preaching of the gospel on the part of the Apostles at the expense of health, happiness, and life, was a work useless and foolish in the extreme. And if it was useless and foolish on the part of the Apostles to suffer so much in preaching the New Revelation, it was equally useless and foolish on the part of those faithful who have endured martyrdom to suffer so much in professing and practicing what it taught.

Why so many thousands living in the Catacombs, why so many thrown to wild beasts in the amphitheater, why so many, throughout the history of the Church, imprisoned for life, burned or beheaded, hanged and quartered? Why might not these heroic souls have chosen some easy form of religion that would have saved them from such tremendous sacrifices, rather than that detailed, stern, inflexible one that cost them the loss of earthly goods, earthly happiness, and even their blood and their life?

Chapter 3

The Conversion of Cornelius
Refutes Indifferentism

The tenth chapter of the Acts of the Apostles gives the narrative of a conversion of a man whose conversion may be regarded as an unanswerable refutation of the theory of indifferentism. I refer to the conversion of Cornelius the Centurion.

The virtues this man practiced before St. Peter saw him, the stern uprightness with which he had acted in accordance with the lights hitherto received, and the succession of miraculous circumstances that led to his conversion make it clear that indifference in matters of religion cannot be reconciled with the gospel of Jesus Christ. The history of his instruction, Baptism, and reception into the Church occupies so large a space in the sacred text that it forms the whole of the tenth chapter of the Acts — a chapter that consists of forty-eight verses. It looks as if the Holy Spirit had penned the lengthy description of this conversion so that it might be a standing record to demolish the flimsy sophistry of those who advocate unrestricted liberty in the choice of a religious creed.

Let There Be No Divisions Among You

The good, moral, upright life Cornelius led before he was baptized by St. Peter, before he had even heard of St. Peter, corresponds with the picture drawn by those who hold that it does not matter what creed a man follows, provided he be a good man after his own fashion. He surely reaches their standard; for he was truly a good man after his own fashion and according to the lights he had received.

He was a soldier, but an exceptionally virtuous one. He had a position in the Roman army. He was centurion of what was called the Italian band. As far as we can see, he was a man in pretty good circumstances, able to live comfortably. And, as to his moral character, it is described in the second verse of the chapter: "A religious man, and one that feared God with all his house — who gave much alms to the people, and prayed to God always." In the language, then, of inspiration, he is declared to be a good man: a man who was full of the fear of God, of the love of God; who spent long hours in prayer, and who divided his substance largely and generously with the poor; whose example had been such that all the members of his household were influenced by it, walked in uprightness as he did, and practiced similar virtues.

Now, what more was wanted? Was he not moving on securely to heaven in his present state? Would he not be sufficiently prepared for a place in heaven by continuing to live as he had lived hitherto? And if the good qualities that are ascribed to him, and the many and exalted virtues he is said to have practiced, had been sufficient to qualify him for a place in heaven, why not leave him as he was?

Perhaps he was following his present lights better than he would follow stronger and fuller illuminations, and corresponding with the graces he was actually receiving more perfectly than he would correspond with more abundant ones. Why, then, not leave him as he was? Why take any further trouble with him?

God, however, did not leave him as he was; *He* condescended to take further trouble with him, if I may be allowed that familiar way of expressing the idea. He sent an angel from heaven to Cornelius. And the angel, in the name of Him who sent him, commanded Cornelius to invite St. Peter, so that St. Peter might come and instruct him and the members of his family as to what they must do. The angel was not content with giving a vague general command. He did not leave Cornelius in doubt as to where St. Peter was to be found. He told him that Peter was in the city of Joppa, described the quarter of the city in which he abode, and mentioned the very house in which he was staying. Cornelius promptly and gladly obeyed this message from heaven. He at once sent three men to Joppa to invite him to his house in Caesarea.

As these three men were approaching Joppa, St. Peter himself had a vision. At the end of this vision, the Spirit of God said to him that three men stood at the door seeking him, that they had been divinely sent, and that he was to go with them whither they would lead him. The following day he set out for Caesarea, accompanied by the messengers who had come to invite him. And the day after he reached the house of the centurion, he instructed him and the members of his household in the true gospel and received them into the one true Church.

Now, here the advocates of indifferentism are on the horns of a dilemma. One of two conclusions they are forced to draw — namely, either God sends His Apostles, and *even* His angels, on useless errands, or it cannot be a matter of indifference to Him what religion people profess. If Cornelius knew God, if he feared Him, if he loved Him — if he loved Him, too, in His poor by relieving those who were in distress—if he spent long hours in prayer, if his life was such that he was styled in inspired language a "just man," why should God send an angel from heaven to him, or why should He send St. Peter from Joppa to Caesarea, to bring to him the light of the new gospel, to administer to him the sacrament of Baptism, and to receive him and his family into the one true fold?

On the other hand, when St. Peter, as an Apostle of the new religion, stood in the presence of Cornelius, and put before him the doctrines of that religion, was Cornelius free to keep any longer to the old form of worship in which he had served God for some time before, and to reject the doctrines that Peter had come expressly to announce to him? Or, was he free to accept some of those doctrines and to reject others?

If he had hesitated, or if he had made it a condition of his being received into the Church that he could go back to his old religion after a time, in case he preferred to do so when he had given the new one a fair trial, and that he was to have the free exercise of his private judgment as to the meaning he was to attach to the gospel truths, would St. Peter have admitted him into the fold of Christ? Certainly not.

Suppose that, after a visit from an angel of heaven; after there stood in his presence an Apostle who had been divinely instructed in a vision to come to him; when it was clear as noonday that it was God's will that he should abandon his old religion and take to the new—suppose that, in spite of all this, he had persisted in clinging to the old one, saying that it was the one he had been most used to, at least for some time. Suppose he had said that he did not ask for a better, that he did not care for novelties and changes. Suppose he said that he dreaded the wrench that such a change must bring with it, that he shrank from breaking with relations and friends, that he feared to incur their dislike, that he might lose his position in the Roman army, that such a step might reduce him and his family to penury, and that, in consequence of these many grave and well-founded fears, he had made up his mind to remain—that he would keep in the old lines, pray as much as he had prayed before, give alms more abundantly still, and do good to all within his reach.

Now, had he reasoned thus and acted thus, and remained in his old religion, while heaven's light flashed upon him with such overwhelming brightness that he saw as clearly as he saw the sun in the heavens that it was wrong to remain in it any longer, would that old religion, and his many virtues, and his many prayers, and his abundant alms have availed him for heaven? No; God had now revealed to him the creed that He commanded him to accept, and he (Cornelius) was not free to put it aside and to follow some other creed instead. He might pray; he might profess to live in the fear of God; he might give all his substance to feed the poor—all would be in vain, unless he gave up his old form of worship, which for *him* could no longer be right, and adhere to that new faith that God, through His angel and His Apostle, had shown him to be the true one, and the only true one.

"Without faith it is impossible to please God."[15] The application of this to current events is already implied, in the supposition I have made with regard to Cornelius, in the event of his having failed or neglected to take the course that he had the happiness to follow.

Before entering upon this application, however, I feel I ought to ask the reader's indulgence while I digress for a short time from the main line of argument. I have less hesitation in asking

[15] Heb. 11:6.

this permission, as the application itself, although it is a slight departure from the direct line of demonstration, embodies, nevertheless, a further refutation of the pernicious system against which I am arguing.

A man, belonging to some non-Catholic denomination, seeing the number of rich, respectable, educated people who leave the ranks of Protestantism and enter the Catholic Church, may become unsettled in the creed he has hitherto professed. He begins to have doubts, and serious ones, as to whether that creed is right or wrong. In spite of the prejudices generated by early education, in spite of those popular calumnies that taught him in his boyhood and early youth that any religion was better than the Roman one, that all churches were good enough *except* the Roman Church, he has, nevertheless, a sort of incipient, although reluctant, leaning toward the faith that that Church teaches.

Natural motives incline him to remain where he is; something abnormal within him (which he cannot explain to himself) impels him in another direction. He stands bewildered in the clash of so many contending, antagonistic creeds; his reason tells him that all cannot be right, that one only can be right, and he is quite uncertain whether he belongs to the one that is right or to one among the many that are wrong. He doubts more seriously every day.

Well, such a man either seeks to have his doubts cleared up or he does not. If he is sincerely eager to find a solution of them, he will set the right way about it, i.e., he will put himself to the trouble of inquiring, of reading, of consulting; he will pray with earnestness, and with his whole heart, for light from on high; and if he continues to pray earnestly and heartily for light, light is sure to come. The darkness of error and the mists of doubt will gradually disappear. No angel may be sent to him from heaven, and no Apostle of the true Faith may be divinely instructed on earth to come to him; but the light of reason and the light of revelation combined may show him—and show him so clearly that he can no longer have any rational doubt about the matter—that his present religion is wrong, and that the one he was taught in his younger years to ridicule and to hold in detestation is the right one, and the *only* right one.

The course he is bound to follow under these circumstances is evident. He is bound to take, energetically and promptly, the final step that will lead him into that Church to which the steady light of faith is inviting him. The same grace that is a star to guide him is meant to be also a help to direct his steps in the path it traces out for him. Not to correspond with that grace, which is at once both light and strength, is to abuse it, and to abuse it is to run the risk of losing it forever; for no man has control over the length of time he is to live or the measure of grace he is to have; and the worst way to get grace in the future is to throw away the grace that is given in the present.

I say he is bound to follow, promptly and energetically, the light that is made to shine upon him and to use the strength that is divinely given him, for God does not give His supernatural helps in vain. When He communicates His lights and His strength, He expects, and He has a right to expect, that they will be used for the purpose for which they are bestowed. And He will demand at the Judgment Seat a rigorous account from those who, through apathy, cowardice, or caprice, shut their eyes to His light or waste those helps that are meant to strengthen them on the way to the true fold.

Such a man may pray a great deal and may perform acts of heroic penance. He may speak with the tongues of men and of angels; he may distribute all his goods to feed the poor. His portrait may hang in every drawing room; his bust or statue may be found in every place of public resort. He may wield a wide influence among his fellow men; he may have the good testimony of all who know him. He may be a useful, beneficent, benevolent member of society; he may be the very ideal of a philanthropist. He may impress all who come in contact with him that he is a good man after his own fashion. Yet all this will fail to save him if he refuses or neglects to enter that Church that he sees in the irresistible light of faith to be the true one, and the only true one. Without faith it is impossible to please God.

Which Church it is to which his star must guide him, if he faithfully follows, we shall determine later on, in the second part of this book, when we discuss the external marks that must necessarily belong to the true Church, and can belong to her alone.

This leads us to the further treatment of the second part of our supposition, i.e., to consider in detail the position of the man who does not seek a solution of his doubts and who strives to drown the voice of conscience by endeavoring to argue himself into the conviction that good works with any form of Christian belief are a sufficient qualification for the kingdom of heaven.

In spite of his efforts to stifle the voice of conviction, his doubts become graver every day, for he cannot help noticing the stream of conversions that is constantly flowing into the Catholic Church. He observes that every year several men of standing, of great ability, of varied learning, leave the Protestant and embrace the Catholic communion. He understands perfectly well that they cannot be doing so from motives of self-interest. He has penetration enough to perceive that in taking such a step they have nothing to gain in a temporal point of view, but everything to lose. He has heard repeatedly that many of them made the change with the certain knowledge that they would lose in consequence their family inheritance, a rich living, an annual income, a lucrative business, a good situation, a means of livelihood; and that they would be disowned and cast off by their nearest and dearest relatives, have to break some of the fondest family ties, incur the displeasure of many cherished friends, and lose the respect of large numbers of old and highly esteemed acquaintances.

He looks at some of the living prominent dignitaries of the Catholic Church in England, and he finds that the history of what they were in the not very distant past is still fresh in the memories of all. That contemporary history tells him that some of the greatest intellects that England has ever produced, that some of the brightest stars that ever shone in the English Protestant church, have in this century abandoned her, and have given their life, genius, heart, soul, and whole being to another Church.

That same history makes it clear to him that these great men did not give up Protestantism without counting the cost. Numberless difficulties stared them in the face — difficulties that would have appalled and unnerved men of less force of will, or would at least have made them try to find principles of expediency to baffle conviction. And souls less brave and hearts less courageous might have succumbed before getting even halfway over the dark waters that separate Protestantism from Catholicism.

They had England at their feet while they remained members of the Establishment; on the other hand, they felt as if they themselves must ever sit at the feet of the humblest members of the priesthood of the communion they were embracing. The high places, to which the Catholic Church was in time to lift them, were still far below the horizon, could hardly be dreamt of (at least by themselves) as things within the range of possibility. They could not foresee the glories that were to crown their courage and make them shine as beacons in the Church of their adoption. The panorama they had to contemplate was, from an earthly point of view, dark beyond description. There was the loss, not merely for a time, but forever, of the high place they had hitherto occupied; the loss of revenues; the loss, too, of the prestige with which fame had already invested their name as champions of the faith they had till then professed; the sacrifice of prospects that made the highest elevations in the Protestant hierarchy far more than probable. On the other hand, there was nothing to look forward to in the Church to which they were submitting but a position of insignificance, crosses, humiliations, perpetual self-denial, and a life of comparative obscurity.

Such the contrast between the fascinations of the delightful life they were renouncing, and the stern rigors of the life of abnegation for which they girded themselves up, when they resolved to take the course in which unchanging conviction was irresistibly drawing them. They had all the merit of that heroic, unlimited self-sacrifice that their will cheerfully embraced when they took the step that severed them forever from the church of their family and lodged them safely in the bosom of the old Church of Rome.

Our friend (who doubts) philosophizes on the conversion of men such as I have been describing. He feels that nothing but the force of conviction, deep and irresistible, could have led them on in this course, could have made them brave such dangers and nerve them for such sacrifices. It occurs to him, too, that if men of such undoubted uprightness, such ability, such learning—men who were so conversant with the question of religion, who were thoroughly qualified to compare the relative merits of different creeds, made up their minds in the face of such formidable obstacles to abjure the church in which they had been brought up and to make their submission to another — then other men of less ability, of less knowledge, and of fewer opportunities of judging, and who were brought up in the same church, ought at least to doubt.

It may have been in reasoning of this kind that his own first doubts had their origin. And since the day when he first became unsettled in the creed of his family, the news of each successive notable conversion has tended to render his doubts more disquieting and more perplexing. He feels impelled to draw the conclusion that those great, able, learned, religious-minded men, who had so many motives to bind them to the church of their birth and early years, would never have renounced her at the cost of such sacrifices, if they had entertained the idea that they could have saved their souls equally easily, or saved them *at all*, in the religion taught by the church they were abandoning.

This process of reasoning may lead him still further, and may incline him to draw the additional inference that if other members of the Establishment, who have remained listless in their doubts for years, had applied their mind to the search after the true Faith with that energy and indomitable perseverance with which they give themselves up to temporal pursuits, a far greater number would have followed in the path traced out by those heroic souls who have so nobly and so courageously sacrificed everything in their glorious search after the truth.

Such are his doubts; such are the facts that have generated them; such are the reflections that have increased them. Still, in *his* case they lead to no practical result. And it is his own fault that they do not. He can reason cleverly enough about the conversion of others and speak eloquently about the conclusions that such conversions ought to incline people to draw. But, although he is full of uncertainties and perplexities himself, he takes no means to have them cleared up. He is tossed about on the ocean of error, and he makes no effort whatever to get on the dry and firm land. Nor can it be argued, in extenuation of this culpable apathy, that he is ignorant of the dangers that surround his present position. He has no difficulty in realizing the gravity, the vital importance, of the point at issue. He knows that religion has to do with the soul, and that the soul is immortal — that with regard to himself it is a question of eternal life or eternal death; and that in reference to God it is a question of serving Him according to the form of worship He has prescribed or some other form of worship at variance with the one on which He has set the seal of divine sanction.

All this he understands; and he fully understands, moreover, the terrible consequences that must attend his want of decision. Although harassed by so many disquietudes and perplexities about matters of religion, he nevertheless enjoys a sort of lethargic peace of soul. While his conscience is oppressed by a multitude of doubts, he chooses practically to ignore them. And if his state of mind is analyzed, it may be described in this form: "I have serious doubts as to the truth of the religion which I nominally profess. I have various reasons for thinking it is not the religion of Christ. I feel unaccountably and irresistibly drawn to another that I have been taught hitherto to despise and to hate. I am quite uncertain whether I am serving God in the right way or the wrong way; and although I am pretty sure I could find out for certain which is the religion in which He wishes me to serve Him if I made the effort, still I will give myself no trouble about it. I know that I ought to inquire, but inquiry is irksome and inconvenient, and if once begun and followed up, it may show me the necessity of making changes from the very thought of which I shrink with horror. Many good men, who are as much bound to inquire as I am, hold that it is a matter of no consequence what form of Christian belief a man professes, provided he be a man of good works. I will remain as I am. I will keep to the creed I was brought up in. I will do as much in the way of good works as I can. I will lead as good a life as possible. And, as to matters of faith, I will take my chance."

This may not be recognized as expressing the state of mind of a certain class of indifferentists, but I think it will be generally admitted that it expresses the state of mind of many. Now here we are engaged in a hand-to-hand combat with our opponents. The defenders of the system of indifferentism, if true to their principles, will hold that this man is quite secure as far as religion is concerned, that he is a good man after his own fashion, and that he has nothing whatever to fear in regard to the world to come.

I maintain that such a man cannot possibly be a good man in God's sense of the word good so long as he remains willfully and apathetically in the state of doubt in which he is living at present. He lacks the very foundation of supernatural goodness, i.e., that firm, unswerving faith, without which no superstructure of supernatural virtue can be raised. His faith, shifting like the sands of the beach, is equivalent to no faith at all. It means everything, and it means nothing; for it means nothing definite. In the secret of his heart, he sets more value on a creed to which he is supposed to be antagonistic than he does on the one that he nominally professes. And yet he has not the courage or the strength of will to enter upon a search after the solution of his doubts. Self-interest, human respect, craven fear, downright apathy, and sheer indifference prevent him from doing so. The things of time absorb nearly all his attention; he has none to give to the settlement of the question on which his eternal state depends. He willingly takes an immense deal of trouble in arranging the affairs of his house, of his family, of his business; in seeking after the situation, occupation, or work that brings the largest wage; in attending to an infinity of trifles. Yet he takes no trouble at all (although he is harassed by constant misgivings about the matter) in assuring himself whether he is doing rightly or wrongly that greatest and most important of all duties—the duty he was sent into the world to do—the duty of serving God. "Fear God, and keep His commandments; for this is the duty of all mankind."[16]

Can we say that the man who attaches so little importance to God's service that he does not care whether he is serving Him in the way that He approves of, or in a way that He condemns, is practicing in any degree that holy fear spoken of in the inspired language that I have quoted?

Does not the first precept of the Decalogue forbid not only the worship of strange gods, but also the worship of the *true God* in a way that is false and wrong? On what foundation then can that man rest the confident hope of being eternally saved who has good reason to believe that he is not worshipping his Creator according to the fashion He has divinely revealed, but according to a bundle of erroneous doctrines and empty rites that have had their origin in the pride and obstinate opinionatedness of novelty-seeking men?

Is God likely to give heaven to those who will not condescend to inquire which is the road that leads to it?

No. Heaven is the greatest reward that in His omnipotence He can bestow. He will never give it to the man who doubts seriously whether he is walking in the way that leads toward it

[16] Eccles. 12:13.

or the way that leads *away from* it, and who does not think it worth his while to make inquiries, even though he has easy and ample opportunities of doing so. If it still be urged that he is a good man after his own fashion, I answer, "That may be; but he is not a good man after *God's fashion*, and on that everything depends." That moral goodness that God demands as a qualification for heaven can never be found in the soul that is oscillating (entirely through its own fault) in vague, perpetual uncertainty, or that is deliberately stifling doubts instead of continuing to inquire with a view to finding a solution to them.

Hence, I hold that the very terms in which the theory of indifferentism is enunciated are sophistical at least, if it is a question of a man into whose mind has come a reasonable suspicion that he is wrong. For that system supposes something as *proved* that is *not* proved, that never *can* be proved, for the simple reason that such a thing is an impossibility. It supposes that a man *can* be a good man, even according to the divine standard of goodness, although he is in constant willful doubt whether he is offering to God a worship that is agreeable to Him or a worship that He must disown and reject. And *can* that great God, who is just and holy and true, ever look upon as good the man who lives day by day in grave doubt, in sheer indifference, whether he is glorifying Him by believing what is true or insulting Him by professing a creed that he has good reason to believe may be false?

God is the God of truth. He necessarily must love truth; and by the same law of His Divine being, He must bear an everlasting and unchanging hatred to what is contrary thereto. The striking words of Cardinal Manning of Westminster in reference to this are appropriate here. Alluding to a kindred subject (i.e., "Rationalism the Legitimate Consequence of Private Judgment"), he says:

Greater things than argument are at stake — the honor of our Lord and the eternal salvation of souls. How great is the dishonor, of which men think so little; as if truth were a sort of coin that they may stamp and change and vary its die and fix its value, and make it in metal or paper as they will! They treat the truth as one of the elements of human barter, or as an indulgence which a man may hold and use for himself alone, leaving his neighbor to perish. This is truth *to me*; look *you* to what *you* believe.

What dishonor is this to the person of our Lord?

Picture to yourselves this night upon your knees the throne of the Son of God: cherubim and seraphim adoring the glory of Eternal Truth, the changeless light of the Incarnate Word, yesterday, today, and forever the same; the heavenly court replenished with the illumination of God, the glorified intelligences, in whose pure spirit the thought of falsehood is as hateful as the thought of sin.

Then look to earth on those whom the blood of Christ hath redeemed; look on those who in this world should have inherited the faith; look at their controversies, their disputes, their doubts, their misery; and in the midst of all these wandering, sinning, perishing souls, look at those who stand by in selfish, cold complacency, wrapping themselves in their own opinion, and saying, "This is truth to me."

Think, too, of the souls that perish. How many are brought into the very gulf of eternal death through uncertainty? How many, as every pastor can tell you, souls are torn from the hand which would save them by being sedulously taught that the deadliest sins have no sin in them; by the specious and poisonous insinuation that sin has no moral quality; how many souls have first been sapped in their faith as Satan began in Paradise: "Yea, hath God said?" (That is, "God hath not said.")

This is perpetually at this hour going on around us; and whence comes it? Because men have cast down the Divine authority and have substituted in its place the authority of men, that is, of each man for himself.[17]

I now return to the argument drawn from the conversion of the centurion: and I return to it to answer an objection. I am well aware that the patrons of indifferentism will appeal to a certain portion of Acts 10 as containing a vindication of their theory. They quote the thirty-fourth and thirty-fifth verses as a clear and explicit defense of it. In these verses we find St. Peter, after hearing from the lips of Cornelius an account of the wonderful way in which he had been visited by an angel and commanded to send for him, giving expression to his thankful admiration of God's loving providence in leading pure-minded men into the true Church. These verses run thus: "And Peter opening his mouth said: In very deed I perceive that God is not a respecter of persons. But in every nation, he that feareth Him and worketh justice, is acceptable to Him."[18]

Now, the supporters of indifferentism, looking at these words quite apart from the context and from the exceptional circumstances in which they were spoken, seem to think that they warrant almost any conclusion; and they have no scruple in drawing a very wide one. They say (at least some of them say) that it is

---

[17] Henry Edward Manning, *The Grounds of Faith: Four Lectures Delivered in St. George's Church, Southwark* (London: Burns and Lambert, 1852), 95–97.

[18] Acts 10:34–35.

evident, from this emphatic declaration of the Apostle, that God does not care what a man is, in point of religion—that He is quite indifferent whether he is a Jew or a Gentile, a Pagan or a Turk, a Presbyterian, a Protestant, a Ritualist, or even a Roman Catholic (if you will), provided he be an honest, straightforward, benevolent, charitable man. Let us see if there is anything in the verses in question to justify this bold reasoning.

Can these words of St. Peter be construed, even by the subtlest understanding of them, into a vindication of the theory of indifferentism? No, certainly not.

For, quite apart from their true meaning, as made evident by the context, the very circumstances even in which they were spoken embody an unanswerable refutation of any such theory. If God were indifferent as to what form of worship His creatures paid Him, then St. Peter's visit on that occasion to Cornelius was useless: his long journey of more than a day from Joppa to Caesarea was useless; the journey of the three men who traveled so far to invite him was useless; the coming of the angel from heaven was useless; the truths Peter announced to him were useless and would have served the purpose quite as well if they had been but a repetition of the old doctrines of the synagogue, or a rehearsal of those fragments of revelation that were already familiar to Cornelius; the Baptism was useless, an idle ceremony that might have been very conveniently replaced by some of the old rites of the Jewish ceremonial. In such a supposition these long journeys and the consequent fatigue, the preparatory instructions given to the centurion and his family before their reception into the Church, the performance of the sacred functions by which they were made members of the Church—all this might have been dispensed with; and so all parties might have been spared a great deal of unnecessary trouble.

The Conversion of Cornelius Refutes Indifferentism

But can we conceive a God of infinite wisdom, who must have an end in everything He does, going beyond the lines of His ordinary providence, working great miracles, employing so many intermediate agents — i.e., servants, Apostles, angels — to lead a man who was already acceptable to Him to a knowledge of a certain definite creed if he cared so little about matters of faith as the advocates of indifferentism would have us believe?

Is not the reason why these propagandists of broad Christianity give to the passage in question so free and wide an interpretation patent to every reasonable man who thoughtfully investigates the matter? Is it not this? They would have it that God must be indifferent about religion, just because *they* are disposed to be indifferent about it themselves. They paint Him not according to the dictates of intimate conviction but according to the bent of natural inclination; and they cling to indifferentism as a creed, not because they believe it is one that is particularly calculated to give Him glory, but because it is one that is particularly suited to their own convenience. It presupposes little restraint, although that is quite as much as they are disposed to bear. It is an excuse for a religion, while it leaves them free to believe what they like and, with regard to many points, perhaps to do what they like. In point of convenience, there is nothing that has the resemblance of a Christian creed that can be compared with it. It saves people from the reproach of being absolute unbelievers, while it gives them unlimited latitude both as to articles of faith and as to the laws of moral conduct.

In fact, it may be said to be diluted idolatry; for those who profess it make God not what He is, but what they wish Him to be — that is, as careless and indifferent about His religion as is the most careless and indifferent among His creatures.

But now, having considered the circumstances in which the words were spoken, let us sift the meaning of the words themselves. "In very deed," said St. Peter, "I perceive that God is not a respecter of persons. But in every nation he that feareth Him and worketh justice is acceptable to Him" (Acts 10:34–35).

The real meaning is evidently the following:

- *First*, God does not exclude the Gentiles from the gifts of faith and of grace and that He is as willing to receive Gentiles as Jews into His Church.

- *Second*, while He is free to give or to withhold from men the gifts of His grace, which are quite gratuitous, He at the same time has no regard to a man's race, or lineage, or pedigree, or country, or nationality, when there is question of the distribution of those gifts; in other words, that being a member of a particular race, or a native of a particular country, is not demanded by Him as a prerequisite for becoming acceptable to Him or for finding favor in His eyes.

- *Third*, suppose that a man knows God and fears Him, and leads a just life according to the supernatural lights that are given him, and does the works of justice with the aid of divine grace according to his present knowledge of religion. If, while he is yet in invincible ignorance that there is any other religion that is true, or, at all events, that there is any other that is better than his own, and if he is in such a frame of mind that if it were made evident to him that his old religion can be no longer right for *him*, he would be quite willing to abandon it and quite willing, on the other hand, to embrace another as soon as he became absolutely certain it was the divine will, he should do so — then such a man, whether he was born in Judea or Galilee or, like Job, in some heathen land, shall find favor with God.

This *must* be the meaning of Peter's words, for it is evident that Cornelius himself is the ideal Peter is describing. Peter is contemplating a man whose circumstances in regard to religion, whose tone of mind, and whose dispositions of heart resembled those of the centurion. And hence the widest conclusion that must be drawn from his words is that God looks with favor on those who live in holy fear and lead a just life according to their lights, as Cornelius did, and who, having no knowledge of a better way of serving Him at present, are ready to adopt a new and a higher form of worship as soon as it is His good pleasure to reveal it to them.

It is to people who act in accordance with their lights in this way that St. Thomas Aquinas alludes when he teaches that it is to be held as *most certain* that God will either, by some interior inspiration, reveal to them what must be believed for salvation or send them some preacher of the Faith, as he sent St. Peter to Cornelius, rather than let them perish through want of faith. His words are:

> Thus, if someone so brought up followed the direction of natural reason in seeking good and avoiding evil, we must most certainly hold that God would either reveal to him through internal inspiration what had to be believed, or would send some preacher of the faith to him as he sent Peter to Cornelius.[19]

[19] St. Thomas Aquinas, *Truth*, 3 vols., Library of Living Catholic Thought (Chicago: H. Regnery, 1952), Q. 14, art. 11, ad. 1.

St. Thomas is treating the case of a man who lives in a place where none of the ordinary or natural means of attaining to a knowledge of divine revelation are to be found. The conversion of Cornelius is, indeed, a striking illustration of the truth of the teaching of this great Doctor of the Church.

But the meaning of the verses in question will become still clearer if we look at the matter from another point of view. Suppose that St. Peter, as soon as he reached Caesarea, perceived that Cornelius, in the short interval between the vision of the angel and his own arrival at his house, had changed his mind again and had begun to resist God's will, even though it had been so clearly manifested to him. And suppose that he declared to Peter that although he knew with absolute certainty that the religion Peter came to announce to him was now the only true one — that it was the divine will he should embrace it *at once*, and that it was wrong for him to follow the old one any longer — and still, having regard to the tremendous temporal difficulties that, for a man in his position, stood in the way, he could not think of making the sacrifices that such a step demanded. Would St. Peter, in such a supposition, have spoken words that implied that Cornelius was there and then acceptable to God? Every reasonable man must answer no; for although Cornelius had been (or in case he had been) in the divine favor until then — until the hour came when there was question of corresponding with or rejecting the signal grace then offered — he would have sinned the moment he willfully and persistently rejected it.

And his sin would have been the particularly great sin of the man who, while heaven's light was shining upon him with its brightest rays to show him what was false on one side and what was true on the other, chose falsehood in preference to truth, and did so from motives of self-interest, and in open resistance to God's will.

Until the apparition of the angel, or a little before, Cornelius, although knowing the one true God, and having implicit faith in Christ the Mediator, had been living in invincible ignorance that there was a higher and a holier religion than that which he was practicing; but that ignorance had begun now to be vincible. The announcement that the promulgation of the gospel of Christ had been made at Jerusalem on the day of Pentecost was spreading widely. It had already reached several cities of the Roman provinces, and Cornelius had probably heard tidings of it from the Jews with whom he associated at Caesarea. At all events, that gospel had now been promulgated to him, personally, in a manner so wonderful and so miraculous that there was no longer room for any doubt. Had he turned a deaf ear to the truths it announced and the laws it imposed, he would have sinned and lost by his sin the grace he had hitherto possessed, or the favor of God, in whose eyes he had until then been acceptable.

Our opponents are not disconcerted. They hold that the conversion of Cornelius, and the arguments we have drawn from it, do not weaken their position in the least. Although Cornelius knew the true God, they observe, still he had not explicit faith in Christ the Mediator; nor had he been as yet instructed in the fundamental doctrines of Christianity. But we, they urge, are Christians, and as such we believe those great and broad truths on which Christianity is built. We hold, however, that within the limits of those broad and wide fundamental truths, it is lawful to construct several different creeds, and creeds, too, that on many points contradict each other.

This reasoning is easily answered. It carries with it its own refutation. That the sophistry it contains may be more thoroughly exposed and our answer to it appear in clearer light, we must look again at some of the doctrines on which the principal Christian creeds differ, and at the same time keep before our minds the momentous importance of those doctrines.

These creeds differ on the doctrine of the Real Presence of Christ in the Eucharist, on the doctrine of sacramental confession, and on the question of the pope's jurisdiction. They also differ as to whether there is a voice on earth that is infallible when it speaks on certain matters in certain given circumstances.

Now, surely it is a matter of importance whether Christ is or is not truly and really present in the sacrament of the Eucharist, whether confession is or is not the ordinary means instituted by Christ for obtaining forgiveness of the grievous sins committed after Baptism, whether the Supreme Pontiff has or has not universal spiritual jurisdiction over the whole world, and whether he is or is not infallible when he speaks in his character of universal teacher on matters of faith and morals.

Could there be doctrines that affect the interests of men's souls more deeply than these? With this question we proceed to answer the assertion of the indifferentist that within the limits of the broad and wide fundamental truths on which Christianity is built it is lawful to construct different creeds, and creeds even that on many points contradict each other.

What is Christianity? We do not ask for an elaborate definition drawn from any theological treatise. Better not to use such, perhaps, since the authority of the theological school from which it issued might be questioned. We shall take the usual or common definition or description found in almost every dictionary, which is to this effect: Christianity is the religion taught by Christ.

Now, the religion taught by Christ was one in its beginning; it has been one ever since; and it must ever remain one to the end of time. It cannot be two. It cannot differ from itself; if it could, it would not be Christ's. As there is only one true Baptism, says St. Paul, one true Savior, one true God and Father of all, so there can be only one true faith. "[Take care] to keep the unity of the Spirit in the bond of peace. One body and one spirit, as you are called in one hope of your calling; one Lord, one faith, one Baptism, one God and Father of all, who is above all, and through all, and in us all."[20]

In other words, Christianity, as it signifies the religion revealed by Christ, means truth. For Christ is the God of truth, who cannot speak a lie. And truth is one: it is something pure and simple. It is not a compound consisting of various elements, some of which are true and others false. It can admit no alloy of falsehood without losing its essence, without ceasing to be what it is. Light and darkness cannot coexist; heat and cold cannot be found in the same place at the same time. Falsehood and truth cannot be built together on Christ, who, as the God of truth, is the foundation on which His religion rests. To affirm, then, that, within the broad and wide limits of Christianity, different creeds and even contradictory creeds may be lawfully built up is simply to affirm that Christ's religion may mean truth and falsehood at once—may be a mixture of what is true and what is false; and that Christ Himself meant it to be such, since, if He did not mean it to be such, it would be against all reason to hold that contradictory creeds may lawfully spring out of it.

But was not that religion true in all its parts, when Christ delivered it to His Apostles, to be propagated throughout the world? And was it not true in all its parts when His Apostles transmitted it to their successors? And was it not that it might

<hr/>

[20] Eph. 4:3–6.

remain true in all its parts, free from all alloy of falsehood, to the end of time, that He promised to send His Spirit, the Spirit of truth, to teach all truth; and promised, too, to be with His Church Himself all days, even to the consummation of the world?

Could He mean, when He revealed those doctrines that were to constitute Christianity, that He left men free to give them contradictory forms according as fancy or inclination prompted? Had even the Apostles themselves any power to change them or to leave people free to believe their opposites, as they thought fit?

And if the Apostles, to whose guardianship they were committed, could not change them in the least bit, how does it appear that any innovator or new evangelist who has come into the world since their day has had any authority to take such liberty with them? What passage is there in the whole range of Scripture from Genesis to Revelation—what has there been handed down in tradition—what is there in the dictates of right reason to justify the assumption that Christ meant to leave people free to draw contradictory creeds out of the religion that He revealed? Does not everything in Scripture, in tradition, in reason point the other way?

I have never heard—you, dear reader, have never heard—no one has ever heard that He said at any time that if men believed the unity of God, the Trinity, the Incarnation, and the Redemption, they might be free about all the other dogmas of His revelation.

But quite independently of reasoning of this kind, the statement is refuted from the very words in which it is made. It leads to conclusions the most absurd. To say that, within the limits of the great fundamental doctrines of Christianity, there is room for different creeds, and creeds that on many points contradict each other, is hardly anything less than a contradiction in terms.

For if such liberty is allowed, Christianity can never have any limits at all. In other words, while the theory of indifferentism may be said to have certain limits to begin with, it has none whatever to end with. It can be expanded to any degree that its upholder wishes, be stretched out indefinitely, and be made to mean anything and everything, or nothing, according to men's whims, fancies, caprices, private judgment, or most foolish eccentricities. There is no restrictive or restraining element in it to check its course.

It is necessarily progressive, changeful, variable.

Freedom of opinion is its principle of life; and freedom of opinion has never recognized any limits in the past, nor is there any hope that it will ever recognize any in the future. The only sphere in which it finds itself at home is illimitable space. There is no anchor to keep it within fixed distance. It is like a puny boat, unfastened from its moorings, swept over the ocean by the rage of the tempest, without steersman, without rudder, without chart, at the mercy of every wind and wave.

Here is the secret why the religion of the Reformation has been divided, and subdivided, and resubdivided into numberless sects. It claimed the right of liberty of opinion, of individual preference; it repudiated the idea of being bound to obey any controlling or authoritative voice that could keep it within definite lines. Hence, its doctrines, like circles on the water, became wider and wider as time went on. These doctrines are expanding still every day; and it is not unreasonable to say that the only thing that will put an end to their constant expansion will be the day of general judgment.

But perhaps we shall be told that even in the Church of Rome, which boasts to be so clear and definite in her teachings, liberty of opinion with regard to certain matters of doctrine is allowed, and that in all such matters members of her communion may hold different and even contradictory views. Why, then, condemn in another Church what we approve in our own? Is it not unfair to deny to others a right that we, to a certain extent, make use of ourselves?

What is the difference, ask our opponents, between our system and that followed by the Church of Rome? Is it not this, that whereas *she* marks off the limits of liberty of opinion at a certain point, we make those limits a little wider? She gives a certain amount of latitude; we give a little more. The difference, therefore, is a difference, not of kind, but of degree.

We shall not seek to evade the difficulty. We shall meet it fairly, face-to-face. And we say at once it is not a difference of degree, but an essential difference of principle between the Catholic Church and non-Catholic churches. Catholics recognize the infallible voice of the Church as the divinely established means of securing unity in faith, by fixing the limits of free thought and of necessary faith. But non-Catholics sanction the right of private judgment, which is a principle not of unity, but of division and diversity.

We readily admit that there are certain things in which the Catholic Church allows her children liberty of opinion. But the very lines within which she circumscribes that liberty may be regarded as an additional, although an implicit, proof of her truthfulness. She marks out clearly the limits up to which liberty may go, beyond which it must never go. "Thus far," she says to her children, "you may go in the exercise of freedom of opinion, but no further."

She defines, too, with equal clearness, the sphere within which necessary faith is demanded, and demanded under penalties of the gravest kind. And so authoritative is her voice, and so distinctly does she draw the lines that mark the boundaries both of liberty and of obligation, that if one of her own children persistently held that there was no liberty of belief where she granted it, she would cease to regard him as a member of her communion and would brand him at once with the mark of heresy. Nor would she be less stern in pronouncing upon him the sentence of excommunication if he obstinately refused to submit his understanding to any of those great and distinctly revealed truths that she binds her members, under pain of heresy, to believe. More than this; if, in order to meet some dangerous innovation, she brings a certain doctrine into more striking prominence, and clothes it in a new garb, although an old truth, so as to meet the heresy it is meant to combat and to crush, any of her members persistently refuses to subscribe to her definition, she condemns him at once in her most emphatic terms and cuts him off unhesitatingly from her communion.

Surely there is a great difference between a religion that is secured by bulwarks such as these against the assaults of rationalism and a religion that, I may say, consists of nothing else but rationalism, which is made up of those favorite doctrines that free inquiry, guided by taste and inclinations, leads a man to choose as his formula of belief. Wide indeed is the distance that separates the man who belongs to a Church that, under penalties such as I have named, demands submission to her teachings, from the man who makes his own fancy and caprice the only measure of his faith and the only standard of his morality. The Church of Christ makes religion something clear, distinct, and definite. Indifferentism makes it something so vague and so variable that it reduces it to nothing. That Church, pointing to her teachings, says to her children: "These are the doctrines that I, in Christ's name, declare have been divinely revealed. These you are bound to believe. In whatever else there may be liberty of opinion, there can be no liberty here."

The system of indifferentism, on the contrary, authorizes its disciples to look through the whole series of Christian creeds just as they would look through the range of stalls at a bazaar. It gives them full freedom to patronize the one that most commends itself to their taste—with the additional privilege of giving it up when they get tired of it and of patronizing some other in preference when fancy, family connection, matrimonial alliance, self-interest, greater convenience, or anything else whatsoever inclines them to do so.

The Church of Christ makes religion consist in God's unchanging revelation. Indifferentism makes it consist in man's ever-changing opinion.

The Church of Christ insists on belief in one definite creed. Indifferentism openly and boldly sanctions the lawfulness of holding as many antagonistic creeds as there are men who hold antagonistic opinions.

Which system has the stronger claim to be judged true?

Chapter 4

∞

The Council of Jerusalem Rejects Indifferentism

The Apostles realized fully that they were bound to guard with jealous care the sacred deposit of faith that had been committed to their keeping. They knew with infallible certainty that that faith was true—true in substance and true in detail. It had come from the lips of Him who was the Fountain of all truth. They could not allow even the least element of falsehood to be mixed up with it.

They had not been long engaged in the ministry of preaching when they had an opportunity of showing their zeal in protecting it against innovation. The Church was still in her infancy when the voice of error made itself heard and sought to destroy her young life. Proud, obstinate men arose who resisted the Apostles, disputed with them, and questioned and even in some points denied the truth of their teaching. These restless innovators maintained loudly and defiantly that the Gentile converts could not be saved unless they superadded the observances of the Mosaic Law to those of the new gospel, and that Judaism was a necessary intermediate step from paganism to Christianity.

St. Paul opposed these positions with all his energy. Peter, James, and John held the same doctrine. The question was one of great moment. The zealots for the Law were moving heaven and earth to carry their point—that is, to make submission to legal prescriptions a necessary qualification for a Gentile's becoming a Christian.

It was a critical time in the life of the Church. The Apostles found themselves placed in circumstances of exceptional difficulty: they must either allow some little falsehood to be mingled with the truths of the gospel, or they must condemn such falsehood and condemn it by a public act, which would have the effect of changing into the bitterest enemies of the Church some who had hitherto been most zealous in extending her sway and in propagating her doctrines.

They foresaw clearly enough the consequences of such public condemnation: a storm of persecution, which the Church, yet young and, according to human appearances, ill able to bear, was sure to follow. Not merely in Jerusalem and Judea, but in the other Roman provinces—indeed, in every part of the world where Jews were found, it would create bitter and persistent opposition. Perhaps those Jews might prevail so far with the Roman authorities as to induce them to prohibit entirely the further preaching of the New Faith.

Such were the difficulties the Apostles had to contend against—such were the dangers they had to encounter. Yet they did not hesitate; they could not allow the gospel of which they were the appointed guardians to be corrupted, changed, or added to. Compromise in things so sacred was out of the question. There could be no communication between light and darkness; truth and error could not live together in the Church of their Divine Master. They must preserve the deposit of faith pure, integral, incorrupt, unmixed with even the least leaven of falsehood.

Although all earth and hell should rage against the rising Church, they must condemn error, condemn it publicly, and condemn it not merely separately and individually, each Apostle by himself—they must condemn it with unanimous voice when met together in sacred council. They were to put on record a public act that would show the people of future times that there was one gospel and one only—that it could not change without ceasing to be what it was in the beginning. And the example they were thus to set in the very dawn of Christianity was to be a standing record throughout all centuries and all generations how error was to be treated—how the gospel of Christ could never bear the innovations of human opinion—how that gospel, pure, intact, unchanged, as it came from the lips of its Divine Author, was the one to be transmitted to succeeding ages, and not some other gospel that was more or less at variance with it.

Although it was inconvenient at the time to hold a council, yet a council was held. It was the first ever convoked in the Church. All the Apostles who could be present took part in it. Some were far away in distant lands teaching and preaching; one, St. James the Greater, had already received the crown of martyrdom. Peter, James the Less, and John, Paul, and Barnabas were there. Peter, as prince of the Apostles, vicar of Christ, the first pope, opened the council and presided throughout. The doctrines and observances that the innovators sought to introduce were examined, discussed, and condemned.

All agreed that such doctrines were irreconcilable with the gospel of their Divine Master. The parting words that that Divine Master had spoken on the day of His Ascension were still fresh in their memories and still sounding in their ears: "Going, teach all nations ... teaching them to observe all things whatsoever I have commanded you." And the Holy Spirit, who had been promised to the Church, who had already come down into her and who was to dwell in her to the end of time, was with them to suggest to them all truth. He guided them in their mode of acting, inspired their deliberations, placed the matter in clear light before them, swayed their decision, and left no room for doubt as to the course they must follow.

They knew with infallible certainty that the Mosaic prescriptions were not among the things that their Divine Master had commanded to be observed; and they knew with equal certainty that that Divine Master would never allow man to add to, or subtract from, or change in any way whatsoever the gospel that He had announced. That gospel was in their hands, and they would guard its identity and integrity at the expense of their lives. They condemned emphatically and unhesitatingly the doctrine that taught the obligation of the Jewish ceremonial law on the Gentile converts:

> Then it pleased the Apostles and ancients, with the whole Church, to choose men of their own company, and to send them to Antioch with Paul and Barnabas: Judas who was surnamed Barsabas, and Silas, chief men among the brethren. Writing by their hands, the apostles and ancients [said]: "To the brethren of the Gentiles that are at Antioch and in Syria and Cilicia, greeting: Forasmuch as we have heard that some who went out from us have troubled you with words, subverting your souls, to whom we gave no commands: it hath seemed good to us, assembled together, to choose out men, and send

them to you with our dearly beloved Barnabas and Paul; men who have given their lives for the name of our Lord Jesus Christ. We have sent, therefore, Judas and Silas, who themselves also will by word of mouth tell you the same things. For it hath seemed good to the Holy Spirit and to us, to lay no further burden upon you than these necessary things: that you abstain from things sacrificed to idols, and from blood, and from things strangled, and from fornication: from which things keeping yourselves, you shall do well. Fare ye well."[21]

Such was the decree. The importance attached to it, the care that was taken to promulgate it, and the effort that was made to secure its observance, may be judged from the verse of Acts in which the history of the council is given: "And he [Paul] went through Syria and Cilicia, confirming the churches: commanding them to keep the precepts of the Apostles and the ancients."[22]

And the same may be gathered from these words: "And as they [Paul and Timothy] passed through the cities they delivered unto them the decrees for to keep, that were decreed by the Apostles and ancients who were at Jerusalem."[23]

The consequences they had anticipated quickly followed. Several apostasies date from the holding of that council. Some, who until then had been among the firmest adherents of the Church, broke with her completely and became her most bitter and determined persecutors. As long as she withheld from

[21] Acts 15:22–29.
[22] Acts 15:41.
[23] Acts 16:4.

condemning Judaizing innovations, they were numbered among her best friends; the moment she pronounced her definition of condemnation, they assumed an attitude of the most desperate antagonism. Her stern, unyielding guardianship of her doctrines brought upon her a persecution from which a slight compromise would have saved her. But she could not purchase peace at the sacrifice of even the least tittle of her teaching.

Now, does not the course of action that this council followed naturally suggest the question: Would the Apostles have acted piously, prudently, or even justly, in thus giving a decision that they foresaw would most likely sever from the Church forever men who had great influence for good or for evil, if they thought it mattered little whether people believed the gospel as our Lord delivered it or believed that gospel when it was added to, diminished, or changed by the innovations of man?

Or, if they thought it mattered little whether an element of falsehood was mixed up with the truth, why not tolerate the different views prevailing as to the obligation or nonobligation of the Mosaic ceremonial law being essential to the Christian Faith, and leave all in peace and free to hold whichever opinion they preferred on this point, provided they professed themselves members of the New Church and continued to fulfill her precepts?

But, further, does not the holding of that council, the circumstances that led to its convocation, and the decisions it put forth suggest another question: Would those Apostles, who condemned so loudly this innovation of Judaism, have approved the modern system of liberalism in religion, of latitudinarianism, of indifferentism, or of whatever other name we choose to give it? Would Peter, James, and John, Paul and Barnabas, or any other Apostle, or all the Apostles, have ratified at that council the doctrine that God was indifferent as to what form of Christian belief people nominally adhered to, provided they were good people after their own fashion? Can any reasonable, serious man hold that the Apostles had it in their power on that occasion to pronounce the decision that, after all, men were not strictly bound to believe the doctrines of the new gospel—that they were quite at liberty to adopt any other doctrines in preference if they chose? If so, it was useless to hold a council at all, useless to teach, useless to preach; and far worse than useless: it was both indiscreet and foolish to evoke such a storm of opposition to themselves.

A theory of religion that would have been condemned in the Church of the first century cannot be regarded as tenable in the Church of the nineteenth. The Church of Christ does not change—if she did, she would not be the Church of Christ. She cannot condemn a doctrine at one period as heretical and sanction it at another as being in harmony with orthodox teaching.

Here, then, in the very outset of Christianity, we see the Apostles in possession of the deposit of faith, holding in their hands the treasure of those revealed truths that their Divine Master meant to constitute His religion. It was a religion that was more precious in their eyes than life itself, and to protect it against the blighting breath of error they were willing to shed their blood and die the martyr's death.

Restless, turbulent, novelty-seeking men sought to tear it from their grasp, to enlarge it, to improve it, to make it square with their individual ideas of Christian obligation, to give it a form of their own. But an authoritative declaration, which bore upon it the impress of divine inspiration, coming from the lips of Apostles assembled in sacred council, made them understand that that religion meant *one* thing, and not *any* thing:

- that it was impenetrable to heresy

- that it was proof against the assaults of error or innovation

- that the opinions of men's private judgment could never find a place in it

- that the privilege of individual preference must ever be discountenanced and repudiated by it as a blasphemous attempt to dissolve the Gospel of Christ and to melt to nothing the doctrines He came from heaven to announce

- that it must ever keep the form and shape and color it had at the beginning

- that it must preserve until the end of time the complete identity it had on the day when it was first confided to their sacred keeping

Such was the attitude of the Church toward heresy and innovation in the first century, while her first Apostles still lived. She had just come fresh from the hands of her Divine Founder. The Holy Spirit had descended upon her on the day of Pentecost, and she was yet in the splendors of His first indwelling. The Apostles, who were the custodians of her doctrines, and who were to bear them to the ends of the earth, were guided by the inspirations of that Divine Spirit; and, thus guided, they acted in the name and spoke with the voice of Him who gave them the great commission to teach and to preach. What *they* approved was approved by *Him*, and what *they* condemned was condemned by *Him*.

Surely we cannot say that in preaching the Gospel, and in condemning error, they went beyond the limits of His authorization.

The Council of Jerusalem Rejects Indifferentism

Surely the course of action that they took in the face of heresy was the course of action their successors were to take in similar circumstances to the end of time. Surely, too, all will freely admit that the Church was right in *their* day; for if she was not right in *their* day, she has *never* been right.

And if in that day, when, in the admission of all, she had still upon her the signs of her divine credentials, she was so intolerant of error, can she afford to be less intolerant of error now? If she felt it a duty to condemn error in the first century, can she let it pass unnoticed in the nineteenth? If she would not allow the least addition to be made to her doctrines while her first Apostles still lived to be her mouthpiece, can she allow the people of the present day to make any change in those doctrines, or to believe what they like or deny what they like?

If so, who gave her leave to change her spirit — to depart from the stern, unyielding rigor with which she guarded the gospel of her Divine Founder in the beginning? Who authorized the successors of the Apostles to be more indulgent toward heresy than the Apostles had been themselves?

Was the Church which would not, and could not, bear the interference of free inquiry in the apostolic age to set the seal of her sanction on that privilege at any future date? Did she not mean the decisive voice of her first council to give the tone to her teachings in this respect down to the consummation of the world?

Suppose that that first council had been convoked to discuss not the question of Jewish or Mosaic observances but the question that is the main subject of this book, i.e., whether one religion was as good as another, whether it could be lawfully held that God did not care which religion people professed, provided they were good people after their own ideas. Could we imagine the Apostles putting a decision like the following: "Knowing that all religions are equal in the sight of God, and foreseeing the different opinions that will prevail among men, and foreseeing, consequently, the difficulty of preserving unity in matters of doctrine, it hath seemed good to the Holy Spirit and to us to declare that all people shall be at perfect liberty to believe that one religion is as good as another — that they shall be at perfect liberty to give any meaning they like to those words of Christ, and to those words of us, the Apostles, which will be handed down to them — that they shall be entirely free, too, to believe as much as they like or as little as they like — that it is a matter of absolute indifference to God what creed a man professes, provided he live up to it."

Now, if the theory of indifferentism, latitudinarianism, liberalism in religion, were tenable, this decision would have sounded perfectly natural on the lips of the Apostles assembled in council. And yet such a decision would have been in absolute opposition to the sacred cause that had brought them together and united their voices in condemning the men who sought to force upon the Church their own private, personal views of religion.

Nay, it would be nothing short of a blasphemy to say that such a definition could come from the lips of those who stood around Jesus Christ on the day of His Ascension and heard from His lips the memorable words: "Going, teach all nations ... teaching them to observe all things whatsoever I have commanded you."

May we not imagine we hear those heroic heralds of the Faith speaking from the benches of that first council chamber to the generations yet unborn — to their successors in the most distant centuries — and saying to them: "As *we* have done, so *you* must do. Guard, protect, defend the deposit of faith against the assaults of innovation, against the dictates of private judgment, against the errors of men, against all the false theories of time, and do not ever allow even the least breath of heresy to rest upon it."

Chapter 5

St. Paul Rejects Indifferentism

I have said that the importance attached to the decree of the council of Jerusalem, the care that was taken to promulgate it, and the effort that was made to secure its observance, might be gathered from the forty-first verse of the chapter in which the history of the council is given. Allusion is made in the verse in question to the mission of St. Paul to the churches in Syria and Cilicia: "And he [Paul] went through Syria and Cilicia confirming the churches; commanding them to keep the precepts of the Apostles and of the ancients" (Acts 15:41).

I may add that the effort made to procure the fulfillment of that decree may be seen in still clearer light in the words of that great Apostle himself to the Galatians. In his epistle to the neophytes of Galatia we find him branding with a withering curse those very same errors that he and his brethren in the apostolate had assembled in council to combat and to crush. And the words of warning and reprehension that he writes on the occasion embody an overwhelming refutation of this flexible system of indifferentism.

Language could not be stronger, clearer, or more scathing than that in which this great doctor of the Gentiles condemns and anathematizes those who sought to introduce a second gospel among the Galatians. He himself had evangelized the Galatians, and had made them members of the one true fold. Scarcely, however, had the seeds of faith begun to germinate and produce fruit among them when the voice of heresy was heard.

Galatia was one of the portions of Asia Minor in which the struggle made by the Jewish converts to have the ceremonial precepts of the Mosaic Law superadded to the gospel of Christ and made binding on the Gentile converts was most violent and most persistent. The Judaizing teachers had succeeded in spreading their doctrines of innovation pretty widely. St. Paul, hearing that some of those whom he had won to Christ had fallen away through the influence of spurious evangelists, wrote an epistle to the Galatians.

The first chapter of that epistle strikes as directly at certain errors of the present day as at those errors it was originally written to condemn. After wishing the Galatians grace and peace from God the Father and from our Lord Jesus Christ, he says:

> I wonder that you are so soon removed from Him who called you to the grace of Christ, to another gospel, which is not another. Only there are some that trouble you, and would pervert the Gospel of Christ. But though we, or an angel from heaven, preach a gospel to you, beside that which we have preached to you, let him be anathema. As we said before, so I now say again: If anyone preach to you a gospel besides that which you have received, let him be anathema. For I give you to understand, brethren, that the gospel which was preached by me is not according to man. For neither did I receive it from man, nor did I learn it, but by the revelation of Jesus Christ.[24]

[24] Gal. 1:6–12.

St. Paul Rejects Indifferentism

I have just implied that this scathing, unqualified condemnation of false teaching strikes as directly at the indifferentism of the nineteenth century as at the errors of the innovators of the first century, who sought to impose useless burdens on the Galatians. May I not express the idea in stronger language still? St. Paul was denouncing men whose chief error was to put forward as binding in conscience certain ceremonial precepts of the Mosaic Law, which had been of obligation in the Old Dispensation, which could never be binding as part of the New, and which were to be entirely abolished in the first century of the Church's history. The aim of those proud zealots was not so much to change any particular article of faith as to add to the articles of faith superfluous, and henceforth useless, ceremonial observances. And if he spoke with such vehemence against those who tried to add to the gospel things that had once been obligatory, and still were lawful, for Jewish converts, would he not have used stronger and more unsparing language still, if such could be conceived, against the abettors of a system that attempts to overthrow the fundamental doctrines of Christianity, and that teaches errors that are in open, palpable contradiction to them? If he hurled such withering anathemas on the heads of the men who dared to add human opinions to the doctrines of the Church, what anathemas would he not thunder against those who should seek to sap her very foundations by proclaiming that it did not matter whether people believed the gospel she taught or some other gospel that denied what she affirmed, and affirmed what she denied?

Can we conceive the man who wrote these words of apostolic censure receiving into the Church, or permitting to remain *in* the Church, Galatians, Romans, Corinthians, Ephesians, Philippians, Colossians, Thessalonians, Hebrews, Jews, or people of any country under the sun, if they persisted in refusing to become her members, or to remain in her communion, except on the condition that they were to have the free exercise of their private judgment, and to be at liberty to accept or to retain this or that particular doctrine according to their own individual interpretation of what is contained in Holy Scripture?

Or can we imagine that if he appeared today before the influential, learned advocates of indifferentism, he would give any assent to, or connive at, the statement that all gospels are good—that one religion is as good as another—that all Christian creeds, although they contradict each other in matters that are of vital importance, if any can be, are equally good, or pretty much the same; and that it is quite immaterial which of them a man embraces as his symbol of faith, provided he shape his life after the one upon which his choice has fallen? They must have a strong imagination indeed who can suppose that such a theory could be endorsed by the Apostle who pronounced such scathing anathemas on the innovators of Galatia.

But, further, it must not be overlooked (for it is a point deserving of very special notice) that he expresses his condemnation of those erring evangelists who sought to force false teachings on the Galatians, a second time, and almost in the same terms. Lest the Galatians might suppose that his words of censure were rhetorical, or that he was writing from human impulse, or that he was rebuking them from a feeling of intense disappointment at their sudden change, and that in calmer moments he would reprove them with less severity—lest any thought of that kind should enter their minds, he repeats, with all the power he can command, and with all the emphasis with which his character of Apostle can invest his words, the same anathema again: "As we said before, so I say now again: If anyone preach to you a gospel besides that which you have received, let him be anathema."

St. Paul Rejects Indifferentism

More than this, as the false teachers, whose sophistry and influence he wanted to make powerless, had quoted (falsely, of course) the authority of Peter, James, and John in support of their opinions, St. Paul pointed to the gospel that he had preached as a thing of such sacredness, such indissoluble unity, such everlasting identity, that neither he nor any of the Apostles, nor even an angel of God, had power to change it in the least item. "I wonder," he says, "that you are so soon removed from him who called you to the grace of Christ to another gospel, which is not another."

He first condescends to style the errors of those heretical evangelists "another gospel," in order that by correcting himself in having dignified them by that name, he may draw more attention to them, and that his overwhelming, crushing condemnation of them may call forth greater horror, and may be more deeply impressed upon their memories. "Which is not another gospel," he adds; for another gospel there cannot be — there can never be. There is but one, the one which we have preached to you — while the world lasts there cannot be another.

Wicked men may strive to pervert it, to add to it, to diminish and explain it away, to mutilate, to corrupt, to change it; but it still remains, and must ever remain, unchanged, unchanging, and unchangeable, like the God whose immutable truths it announces. "Jesus Christ yesterday, and today, and the same forever."[25] "One Lord, one faith, one baptism. One God and Father of all, who is above all, and through all, and in us all."[26]

Some, however, who would fain justify, through the principles of indifferentism, the system of faith that they at present profess (although they have serious misgivings about its truth)

---

[25] Heb. 13:8.
[26] Eph. 4:5–6.

take refuge in a fact that affords anything but grounds for solid argument. When driven from every other position, they fall back upon this as a sort of forlorn hope. They say: "The creed which I now profess was the creed professed by my father; it was the creed of my grandfather, the creed of my ancestors from time immemorial — at all events, since the Reformation; if it was good enough for them, it ought to be good enough for me."

This is weak philosophy indeed.

The many and wonderful conversions to the Catholic Faith that have taken place in England might be regarded as furnishing a sufficient answer to this. But entirely apart from the logic of such events, an answer is easily found.

The fact that a man's religion was the religion of his father, the religion of his grandfather, and the religion of his ancestors for centuries past does not prove that religion to be true. If it was wrong in its beginning, it has been wrong ever since; age cannot have made it right. The transmission of an error from one generation to another cannot change that error into truth. Length of time, under certain given circumstances, may give a prescriptive claim to the possession of property, but no number of years can give error any sort of claim to the submission of man's understanding. A custom may be sanctified by antiquity; but an antiquity equal to the age of the world could not sanctify falsehood or change heresy into orthodox religion.

Falsehood may be polished up, refurbished, gilded, draped in a fascinating sophistry that makes it appear tolerable, plausible, and even commendable in the eyes of the overcredulous and unreflecting; it is falsehood, however, all the while and must remain falsehood to the day of doom.

More than this: if reasoning of this kind justified a man in remaining in the creed he was born in, the Gospel of Christianity could never have been reasonably expected to make any progress. For both the Jews and the Gentiles to whom the Apostles preached might, in such a supposition, have rejected entirely the doctrines of the new Faith. They could have said to those who sought to make the light of the Christian gospel shine upon them that they were quite satisfied with the religion they were already professing, that it had been the traditional religion of their families for centuries before, that they did not deem themselves better than those of their race who had gone before them, and that they could not make up their minds to abandon a form of worship to which their predecessors had clung so long, so faithfully, so persistently, and so scrupulously.

But further: our opponents, by this quasi appeal to the past, are unconsciously opening the way to the argument that, of all others, is the most fatal to the theory they are advocating. For although their present faith has been, in its many and perpetually changing forms, the faith of their fathers for some generations, or even some centuries past, yet there was a time a little further back when it was not the faith of their fathers. From the sixteenth century, Protestantism, or some fragmentary religion that was an offspring of Protestantism, *may* have been the creed according to which the successive generations of their family worshipped; beyond that century it could not have been, for the simple reason that it did not exist. And if it had no existence until *then* and was born into the world only at that date, it was born more than fifteen hundred years too late to be the religion of which St. Paul spoke when he said, "If I or any angel of heaven preach to you a gospel besides that which we have preached, let him be anathema." Cardinal Manning, speaking on "Revealed Truth Definite and Certain" and referring to this last resource of the indifferentist, says:

Well, you will perhaps tell us that you have inherited the faith you hold. The inheritance of faith, that is a Divine principle. We bow before the principle of inheritance. But why did you cut off the entail of your forefathers? Why, three hundred years ago, did you cut off the entail of that inheritance? If it be not cut off, why is the contest? If it be cut off, why was it cut off?

To inherit the faith is the Divine rule. It needs only one thing, infallibility, to secure it. It needs only one support to give it substance and certainty: a Divine tradition flowing from the Throne of God through Prophets, Seers, Apostles, Evangelists, Martyrs, Saints, and Doctors in one world-wide stream, ever deepening, never changing, from the beginning until now. Show this Divine certainty as the basis of your conviction, and then inherit both truth and faith. But the inheritance of opinion in a family, or a diocese, or a province, or nation—what is it? Human in the beginning and human to the end: the traditions of men.

You say you have inherited the faith, and that this is the Church of your forefathers. Go back three hundred years ago and ask the priests of God, who stood then at the altar, how *they* would expound the faith you still profess to hold. Ask them what they believed while they ministered in cope and chasuble.

Go back to the Apostle of England who first bore hither again the light of the Gospel after Saxon paganism had darkened this fair land. Ask St. Augustine what he believed of these words "Thou art Peter, and upon this rock I will build My Church." Give *your* exposition, and ask *all*.

St. Paul Rejects Indifferentism

What would he have taught you of visible unity? What would he teach you of the Church of God? Ask him: Is it one numerically, or only by metaphor? Is it visible, that all men may see the city seated on a mountain, or invisible, that men may weary themselves and never find it? Has it a head on earth representing its Divine Head in heaven? Or has it no head, and may set up many of its own? What would he have taught you of your baptismal creed?

Or that great saint who sent him from the apostolic throne, what would he have testified to you of those doctrines of faith which you are to look upon as errors? Ask Gregory,[27] first and greatest of the name, what he believed of the powers left by the Incarnate Son to His Church on earth; what he taught of the power of the keys transmitted by his predecessors in lineal descent from the hands of his Divine Lord. Ask what he taught of the power of absolution in the Sacrament of Penance; what he believed of the Reality on the altar, and of the Holy Sacrifice daily offered in all the world; of the Communion of Saints ever interceding, by us ever invoked; of the intermediate state of departed souls, purifying for the kingdom of God. Ask Gregory, saint and doctor, to whom we owe the faith, what he taught of those doctrines which you have rejected.

If the disciple and his Master, if he that was sent and He that sent him, were to come now and tread the shore of this ancient river, whither would they turn to worship? Would they go to the stately cathedral, raised by their

---

[27] Pope St. Gregory I (known as "Gregory the Great"), ca. 540–604.

sons in the faith, where even now rests a sainted king of Catholic England? Would they bend their steps thither to worship the God of their fathers, and their Incarnate Lord, from whom their mission and their faith descended? Or would they go to some obscure altar in its neighborhood, where an unknown and despised priest daily offers the Holy Sacrifice in communion with the worldwide Church of God?

If then you claim inheritance as the foundation of your faith, be true to your principle, and it will lead you home. Trifle not with it. Truth bears the stamp of God, and truth changes men to the likeness of God. Trifle not with the pleadings of the Holy Spirit within you; for He has a delicate touch, and sensitively shrinks from willfulness and unbelief.

If truth struggle within you, follow it faithfully. Tread close upon the light that you possess. Count all things loss that you may win truth, without which the inheritance of God's kingdom is not ours. Labor for it and weary yourselves until you find it.

And forget not that if your religion be indefinite, you have no true knowledge of your Savior; and if your belief be uncertain, it is not the faith by which we can be saved.[28]

Although our proper scope is rigid demonstration, yet we may be excused if we make the following little digression to record an example that bears intimately on the phase of indifferentism that we have just been noticing. This little book may (and we

[28] Manning, *Grounds of Faith*, 19–22.

hope it will, largely) fall into the hands of persons outside the Catholic Church who have begun to doubt the truth of their present religion and whose chief objection to further inquiry or nearer approach to Catholic unity is the shrinking, or shyness, or inward movement of human respect that they feel at the idea of giving up the traditional creed of their family.

Let such reflect on the noble and chivalrous answer given by Count Leopold Stolberg,[29] after he became a Catholic, to Frederick William III, king of Prussia,[30] father of the emperor of Germany. Stolberg was a man of unswerving uprightness and of uncommon learning. He read much, studied much, reasoned much, wrote much and well. All Germany was filled with the fame of his learning, of his writings, and of his high-mindedness. He was a good man according to his lights; he followed those lights faithfully.

After mature deliberation, it became clear to him that he was bound to abjure Protestantism and to embrace the Catholic Faith in its stead. He did not hesitate or allow himself to be held back by useless and dangerous delays. He made his submission to the Church of Rome promptly and publicly; and did so in spite of difficulties greater in number, and of a more serious kind, than any that surround the conversions that are taking place around us at present.

The first time he appeared at court after his renunciation of Lutheranism and solemn reception into the Catholic Church, the king said to him in a tone of bitter reproach, "I cannot respect the man who has abandoned the religion of his fathers."

---

[29] Friedrich Leopold Graf zu Stolberg (1750–1819) was a German poet, lawyer, and translator.

[30] Frederick William lived from 1770 to 1840.

"Nor I, sire," replied Stolberg, "for if my ancestors had not abandoned the religion of *their* fathers, they would not have put *me* to the trouble of returning to it."

Here is the right spirit—here is fearless courage of the right kind.

Neither the desire of retaining the king's esteem, nor the fear of losing the king's friendship, could sway this noble-hearted man one iota. He saw that Protestantism meant only latitudinarianism or indifferentism, that it had no foundation to rest upon, that it led to incipient rationalism by bringing revelation down to a level with the law of nature, and that in its further stages it led to atheism. And, seeing this, he broke with it forever and sought admission into the communion of the Church of Rome.

Indifferentism, then, has no firm ground to stand on. It cannot bear investigation. It may appear substantial, firm, fair, and fascinating in the eyes of those who do not care to look beneath the surface, but it breaks and crumbles to pieces in analysis. It would have us believe that God spoke with the view of revealing something and that yet He revealed nothing definite; that He made known some doctrine, and at the same time gave men leave to give that doctrine any meaning they pleased; that He proclaimed some statement as true, and left men perfectly free to believe it was false; that He made a revelation and, while making it, did not care in the least in what sense men received it, or whether they received it at all, or whether they received it in two opposite senses, the one contradictory of the other.

It would have us believe that, while our Divine Lord says faith is necessary to salvation, faith after all is *not* necessary to salvation; in other words, that the statement is true or false according to the standpoint from which it is looked at. It would have us believe that, while God meant something definite when He gave the Ten Commandments through Moses on Mount Sinai, His Divine Son did not mean anything definite at all when, on the Mount of His Ascension, He commanded His Apostles to teach and to preach to the nations the doctrines and precepts they had heard from Him.

It will not allow the Ten Commandments to be subjected to the action of free inquiry or private judgment, but it lets free inquiry and private judgment deal as they like with the doctrines revealed personally, directly, audibly, visibly, by our Lord Himself. It makes the divine message so impalpable, so versatile, so chameleon-like in its changeableness, that, by some inherent, heaven-born property that it possesses, heaven knows how, it necessarily accommodates itself to each fresh mind it meets.

Indifferentism means all this and more. It is a contradiction of man's reason, and it is a contradiction of God's Word. It is a contradiction of the great apostolic commission: "Going, teach all nations ... teaching them to observe *all* things whatsoever I have commanded you."

It is a contradiction of the teaching of the Holy Spirit, who is the Spirit of truth; for it sanctions contradictory statements, and therefore necessarily sanctions falsehood. It contradicts the collective teaching put forth by the first Apostles in council; for the Apostles met in council expressly to condemn error and to stop the inroads of innovation.

It contradicts the teaching of the Apostles taken individually, for St. Paul was only echoing the voice of his apostolic brethren, who had been born into the apostolate before him, when he said: "But though we, or an angel from heaven, preach a gospel to you besides that which we have preached to you, let him be anathema."

Let There Be No Divisions Among You

It is a practical, permanent, persistent contradiction of Christianity. Christianity (I mean orthodox Christianity) may be said to be Christ teaching religion to man. Indifferentism is man explaining away that religion, minimizing it, reducing it to nothing.

Christianity is something supernatural both as to the lights it brings to the mind and as to the laws it imposes on the will. The religion of indifferentism, when analyzed, is hardly anything but an outward, imperfect, and even unfaithful expression of the light of reason, and a repromulgation of the law of nature.

Its natural tendency, therefore (though many of those who profess it as their creed do not, I believe, realize this), is to dissolve all revealed religion and consequently to dissolve Christ. No creed can stand before so powerful a solvent as this. It is an engine of destruction before which all revealed doctrine must fall to pieces.

It tends, as far as in it lies, to loosen every stone in either side of that great arch of Christian truth that spans the universe; nay, it tends to loosen the very keystone of that arch, to bring the whole sacred structure to the ground, to leave the world without a single trace of the divinity or teaching of Jesus Christ, and to reduce it to that state of spiritual chaos whose only, or whose best, religion is the "Unknowable." And indifferentism or liberalism in religion would have brought the world to this state of utter anarchy in matters of faith long before now, had not the edifice of *true* Christianity been built upon a foundation that could never fail and been sustained by an omnipotent, though invisible, hand, that made it proof against all the efforts of innovation and all the assaults of men and of devils.

Where that true Christianity is to be found is now the question.

As many of those who belong to non-Catholic denominations will admit that it is *possible at least* that the creed that they now profess is wrong, I do not think that we do any violence to their feelings when we ask them to pray that, in case they have not the true faith at present, the light of God's grace may guide them into the full and calm possession of it.

Prayer is the way to the true Church.

As the star of the Eastern kings, though its light was intermittent, nevertheless continued to shine with sufficient steadiness until it brought them into the cave of Bethlehem, so the star of grace, which is formed by humble, confident, earnest, and persevering prayer, will infallibly, sooner or later, guide the sincere inquirer into that one true fold in which *alone* Jesus Christ dwells, and in which *alone* He speaks and teaches.

It is in the light of this truth that we desire all outsiders, into whose hands these pages may fall, to read what we shall now put before them with respect to those signs or marks by which that true fold is to be distinguished from every other. We take the liberty of advising them to ask, in the words of Alexander Pope's *Universal Prayer:*

> If I am right, Thy grace impart
> Still in that right to stay;
> If I am wrong, O teach my heart
> To find that better way.[31]

---

[31] *The Works of Alexander Pope Esq.*, vol. 3, *Containing His Moral Essays* (Dublin: printed for George Faulkner Abraham Bradley, and Thomas Moore, 1751), 157.

Part 2

∞

Marks of the One True Church

Chapter 6

∞

The Criteria

There are many who will accompany us thus far. They readily grant all that has been said. They admit that all religions cannot be true—that one only can be true—that all the rest must be false. They admit further that there is a true religion in the world somewhere. This, of course, they are forced to admit; else the gates of hell have prevailed, and Jesus Christ made a promise that He either could not or would not fulfill. And to say either would be to speak with grave irreverence against His omnipotence or fidelity. To assert that He promised to do something that He did not mean to do, or had not the power to do, would certainly be a blasphemy.

When at Caesarea Philippi He spoke the memorable words in which He proclaimed to the world that His Church was to be built on a rock, firm, unyielding, immovable, against which no power of earth or hell could prevail;[32] and when again He declared, just before ascending to His Father, that He would remain

---

[32] "Thou art Peter; and upon this rock I will build my church; and the gates of hell shall not prevail against it" (Matt. 16:18).

with her all days until the consummation of the world,[33] the whole of her future history was present to Him. Nay, the whole future history of the world, in all its varied events, circumstances, changes, revolutions, wars, schemes, intrigues, treasons, schisms, heresies, stood out as clear before Him as the Apostles whom He was addressing. For He was God, to whose infinite knowledge all things, past, present, and future, were equally visible.

Now, would He, or could He, have uttered these solemn promises if He had foreseen there was ever to be a time when His Church would do any deed, or teach any doctrine, or commit any betrayal of trust that would force Him to forsake her, or force Him to allow the powers of error or of evil to prevail over her?

There is nothing in His words, nor is there anything in the sacred circumstances in which He spoke them, to justify any such supposition. His promises are absolute, unconditional, unqualified by any limitation, whether expressed or implied. And surely on such promises we can safely rest the following statement: The Church of Christ existed once on earth; and so surely as she existed *once*, so surely does she exist *still*, in some part of the world or other, or else Christ is not God, or if He is God, He has promised and not fulfilled.

But now comes the question.

The honest, earnest inquirer, who has followed us thus far, will ask: "Which *is* His Church? Where is she to be found? Point her out. Show me how she is to be distinguished among the numberless claimants, all of which arrogate to themselves the prerogative of divine institution. "Here I stand," he continues, "bewildered, amid the din, the clash and clamor of contending, antagonistic sects, each and all of which lay claim to truth. Though in their

[33] Matt. 28:20.

teachings, they are as far apart from each other as the poles, though they are separated by huge mountains of contradiction, yet they all and each profess to be the true Church. What, then, are the marks, signs, tokens, by which I can find out for certain, and without any lingering feeling of doubt, which among them all is the one true Church of Christ?"

Such is the question we have to answer. Such is our search.

We do not begin by saying which is that Church. We shall come to it step by step. And we shall not seek to advance one inch on the way that leads to our conclusion, except by arguments that we think will be looked upon as honest, fair, straightforward, and solid by all reasonable men.

To determine which Church among all is right, we must summon the rival claimants before the bar of plain common sense and examine which claimant has the best, nay, the *only*, claim to be believed as the one true Church of Christ.

It is evident that if Christ established His Church for the salvation of the people of all time, He could not have made her so obscure, so hidden, so mysterious that it would take years of historical research, and a thorough knowledge of the Scriptures from Genesis to Revelation, to find her out. If so, she would be forever beyond the reach of the ignorant and uneducated who would be born outside her pale. He must have meant her to be something palpable, tangible, visible, *strikingly* visible, easily discoverable by all who had not yet discovered her; and, also, easily distinguishable from the spurious, schismatic, and heretical sects that He foresaw would in time rise up around her and strive to supplant her.

His design was that she should be like the city built on a hill,[34] as plain to the sight of the unlettered, who would open their

---

[34] Cf. Matt. 5:14.

eyes and look around them, as to the keen penetrating glance of the scientist. For she could never answer to the purpose of universal salvation for which she was framed, unless her divine credentials were legible to the poor and the rich, the illiterate and the scholar alike.

What are those credentials or marks?

There are several; but they may be reduced to two. At all events two will be sufficient for our purpose. Whichever Church is Christ's must have these two; and she *alone* ever *can* have them.

One is the *mark of unity*, and the other is the *mark of universality* or *catholicity*. All who belong to any Christian denomination will readily grant that whichever Church is Christ's must necessarily have these marks.

Several sectarian denominations recite as their symbol of faith the Nicene Creed which enunciates them: "And I believe in one, holy, Catholic Church." But quite independently of that ancient formula, reason enlightened by faith compels us to the conclusions that it must be so.

Chapter 7

∞

Unity

Whichever Church is Christ's must be one—cannot be two. If she were two, she would not be the one true Church of Christ. This may sound like a truism. I mean, if she taught contradictory statements about doctrines of vital importance, she could not be the one true Church of Christ. For if she taught contradictory dogmas of faith, she must teach falsehood; and Christ, who is the God of truth, and whose voice speaks in her, cannot teach falsehood.

Nor can He dwell, by a perpetual and abiding presence, in any Church that teaches what is false; for His abiding presence is an approving presence, and He can never set the seal of His approbation, either explicitly or implicitly, on any doctrine that is opposed to truth.

For a similar reason, she (whichever Church is Christ's) cannot sanction, permit, or tolerate the use of any principle or privilege that, taking men as they are, necessarily leads to contradictions in fundamental matters of faith; just because she cannot sanction, permit, or tolerate any principle or privilege whose application leads of necessity to falsehood. No reasonable man will hold that she would be Christ's Church if she did. These statements will be equivalent to first principles, in the judgment of all who regard the Church as a work of divine institution.

If we gainsay them, if we refuse to see them in that light, we are unconsciously admitting that her teachings, even before the end of the first century, may have been a chaos of contradictory doctrines, in which it would have been impossible to tell whether the element of truth or the element of falsehood predominated. In fact, to deny them is simply to deny as a mark of the true Church that unity that Christ Himself expressly declared was to be one of her most distinguishing and most striking marks.

At the Last Supper, toward the end of His parting discourse, He raised His eyes to His Eternal Father and prayed that there might be unity among His Apostles and unity among the faithful, who through their preaching were to believe in His gospel. And He not only prayed that unity might bind them all together, but He proclaimed in that very same prayer that He meant that unity to be a proof to the world that *they* were His own flock, and that He Himself had been divinely sent: "And not for them [the Apostles] only do I pray, but for them also who through their word shall believe in me that they all may be one, as Thou, Father, in me, and I in Thee; that they also may be one in us: *that the world may believe that* Thou hast sent me."[35]

Now, would not that prayer have been meaningless if He meant, while He said it, that the Apostles or the faithful, the priests or the people, were to have the free use of a privilege before which all definite revelation would melt away, which would leave them free to give opposite forms to every doctrine He had made known and contradictory interpretations to every word of His that was to remain on record. Or, could He, the God of

[35] John 17:20–21, emphasis added.

unchanging truth, ever have put forth that solemn petition to the Father, if He intended, while He said it, that Peter was to be free to preach one doctrine in Antioch and John the contradictory in Ephesus?

Well, I think we may say that two points have been established: first, the Church of Christ—the Church of the everlasting rock—exists somewhere on earth; second, that Church can neither teach contradictory doctrines of faith, nor approve or tolerate a principle whose use necessarily leads to contradictions in doctrines of fundamental importance.

Now, apply this test to the numberless creeds outside the Catholic communion that proclaim themselves orthodox, and see if they can stand it.

The principle of private judgment, free inquiry, individual preference, as we shall see presently, not merely leads, but, taking men as they are, leads of *necessity*, to contradictions, and to contradictions in even the most important matters of faith; and, consequently, leads of necessity to false conclusions with regard to the most important matters of faith.

But the Church of England, and all the branch churches that have sprung from her, enforce, sanction, or tolerate the use of private judgment. This statement may sound too bold and comprehensive. It is, however, undeniable. Nearly all the members of the Anglican communion will admit it; and the twentieth of those articles on which the Anglican creed is founded plainly professes it. And even the High Church and Ritualistic party, which is loudest in disclaiming it, uses it, and uses it in its most intense form; while those who belong to the Low Church and Broad Church party will not pretend to deny that the Scripture is their only rule of faith, and that private judgment is its interpreter. Besides, those articles, to which all the clergy of the

Establishment are bound to subscribe, are forthcoming to prove that it is so.

In the sixth article it is stated: "Holy Scripture containeth all things necessary to salvation; so that whatever is not read therein, nor may be proved thereby, is not to be required of any man that it should be believed as an article of faith, or be thought requisite or necessary to salvation."[36] And the twentieth article runs thus: "The Church hath power to ordain rites and ceremonies, and authority in controversies of faith; and yet it is not lawful for the Church to ordain anything contrary to God's Word written; neither may it so expound any passage of Scripture so as to be repugnant to another."[37]

Dr. Beveridge, a celebrated Protestant divine, whose teaching is confirmed by other and later writers, guided by these articles, maintains that each individual is bound to look to the proofs of what he specifically believes, and obliged to be a member of his Church on grounds that he himself has verified.

Further remarks on this point are unnecessary, since the principle that each individual must judge for himself, and make out his own system of faith from the Scriptures, is admitted by the members of the Low Church and Broad Church party.

But even the members of the High Church and Ritualistic party, who will not allow themselves to be reproached with professing the principle of private judgment, use it, and use it, as I have said, in its most exaggerated form.

---

[36] Edward Harold Browne and J. Williams, *An Exposition of the Thirty-Nine Articles, Historical and Doctrinal* (New York: H. B. Durand, 1865), 128.
[37] Ibid., 478.

Unity

I will give here my reasons for saying so. Their belief in the past, their change of belief, their present anomalous position, the various phases through which their creed has passed, their stopping within the boundary line that they have now reached, their obstinate unwillingness to move an inch beyond it, makes this clear to evidence. Their gradual approach to that series of dogmas that they at present profess has been an exercise of private judgment all along.

For if, when the hour of change came, they departed from the doctrines of their earlier years and replaced them by doctrines taught by the Church of Rome, was it not free inquiry, individual preference, and private judgment pure and simple, that led them to take that course? Their interpretation of their Anglican position, and of the formularies and doctrines of their church, in a Catholic sense, as contrary to the Protestant sense, that had before so long prevailed—what was all that but the result of private judgment? And their standstill on the line of demarcation that now separates them on one side from their coreligionists, and on the other from the members of the Roman Catholic communion—what is it but a constant, continuous exercise of the same arbitrary choice?

If they move neither backward toward the creed of their early youth, nor forward still nearer to the Church of Rome, it is nothing but private judgment that keeps them where they are. There is no external power, no authoritative tribunal, to keep them there. Their own church—the church to which they nominally belong—is quite passive in their regard. She merely looks upon their state of oscillation, transition, change with the eye of toleration. And *they* give pretty clear proof that they would not listen to her voice, even if she spoke in the tone of authoritative prohibition.

Let There Be No Divisions Among You

They acknowledge no living authority of any kind that can bind them to keep fixedly to the doctrines that make up their present creed. The only real, living, tangible authority they recognize is their own freedom of mind, individual preference, private judgment, which has been their guide throughout, and which, from the day it broke loose from the traditional fragments of Anglican belief, has never submitted to any external control.

And that private judgment, being still free to roam unchecked, being at perfect liberty to change its former decision in a moment, may induce them in the not-far-distant future to discard utterly all the Catholic doctrines they at present profess.

They may tell us loudly that they do not use private judgment in the interpretation of the Scriptures. Well, if they do not pretend to interpret the Scriptures by private judgment, they interpret the ancient Fathers by private judgment, and that comes pretty much to the same thing. Perhaps it is more correct to say that they use private judgment in their interpretation both of the Scriptures and of the Fathers. The field in which they exercise private judgment is in reality broader and wider than that claimed by any other sectaries whatever. While others are content to confine the exercise of this arbitrary right to the Bible, *they* let it loose upon the decisions of the early councils and the writings of the Fathers.

That is, they make certain passages of Scripture give out certain favorite doctrines by an appeal to the interpretations given to those passages by the early Fathers; while, with regard to other passages, they reject entirely the interpretations of those Fathers and follow their own interpretation in preference. If this is not private judgment, it is hard to say what is.

They take up the history of the early councils and the writings of the ancient Fathers, and they find that the primitive Church must have believed this doctrine and that doctrine and that other doctrine. Guided by these venerated records, they give to certain passages in Scripture the Catholic interpretation—an interpretation that the other members of their communion entirely disclaim and emphatically repudiate.

They copy these doctrines into their new creed, just because, in their present temper of mind, such doctrines commend themselves to their private fancy.

Then, suddenly, it is found they are prepared to go only a certain length, and no further, with the early Fathers; although there is quite as much reason, and more, for going the whole way as there is for stopping when they have gotten a certain distance.

While they gladly transfer into their new symbol of faith the doctrine of Confession and of the Eucharist, because they find these doctrines clearly enunciated in the writings of the ancient Fathers, they sedulously keep out of it other doctrines of equally vital importance, and which are expressed with equal clearness by the very same Fathers. If they profess to believe that the priest has power to forgive sin, and that Christ is really present in the Eucharist, on the ground that the early Fathers taught these dogmas, why refuse to believe those very same Fathers when they teach, with equal clearness and equal emphasis, the necessity of being in communion with the See of Rome, and of submitting to its authority, as being an authority that all are bound to obey and from which there is no appeal. If they agree with St. Irenaeus when he speaks words that embody the Catholic doctrine of the Real Presence of Christ in the Eucharist, why not agree with the same Irenaeus when he teaches so unequivocally that it is necessary that every Church should be in communion with the Church of Rome? No words could be clearer than those that this Father of the Church uses when referring to this vital doctrine:

"For it is a matter of necessity that every church should agree with this church, on account of its pre-eminent authority."[38]

What reason can they give for taking in just so much of the dogmatic teaching of the primitive Church as they do take in, and nothing more, and for treating all the rest as a matter of comparatively trivial importance?

Is it not evident that, although they borrow certain materials from the early Church in building up their creed, they are following not her teachings but rather the dictates of their own private judgment and the promptings of their own imagination?

While they disobey the traditions of the Establishment by embracing a belief rejected by most of its bishops and the greater part of its laity, they refuse to obey any other church, except that ideal one that exists in their imagination and can exist nowhere else. I say it can exist nowhere else for no church such as they picture to themselves ever came into actual life.

The ancient one, of which they pretend theirs is the modern realization or semimiraculous resurrection, was in communion with Rome. If, then, they mean theirs to be the identical ancient Church, it must have the Roman pontiff for its head; and since it has not the Roman pontiff for its head, but is a body or part of a body without a head at all, it cannot be the identical old Church.

Their Church is a nebula — it is a structure in the air. It is not God's work; it is their own work — a thing struck out of their own head, created, framed in outline, and decorated in detail by the exercise of private judgment and the caprice of individual taste. Trace the process they follow in its formation, and you will find

---

[38] Irenaeus, *Adv. Haer.* 3, 3, in *The Writings of Irenaeus*, 2 vols., Ante-Nicene Christian Library (Edinburgh: T. and T. Clark, 1868), 261.

this to be the case. They draw a plan in their mind of what they imagine the ancient Church must have been, then they gather fragmentary or isolated doctrines from the early chronicles of the Church of the East and of the West, from the writings of the ancient Latin Fathers and of the ancient Greek Fathers; they introduce a sprinkling of the novelties of the Reformation; they also draw upon certain doctrines of their own invention; and out of these heterogeneous elements they rear their phantom fabric.

Their religion, then, as it exists in its present form, is entirely their own arbitrary creation. It owes its whole being to the activity of private judgment. Hence, *they* are not under *its* control; *it* is entirely under *their* control. They made it when they chose; they can keep it for as long or as short a time as they choose; they can abolish it any moment they deem it prudent or expedient to do so. It was private judgment that called it into being; the same private judgment can annihilate it in the twinkling of an eye.

The church they profess to belong to is either dead or living. If it is dead, it cannot receive their submission, and they cannot obey it. If it is living, it must be the primitive Church *out* and *out*, or it is nothing. Else they must have us believe that the pure, perfect, primitive Church died and disappeared altogether from history for centuries; that the very rock moved away out of sight, too; and that that ancient rock and ancient Church, in all its beauty, perfection, and completeness, emerged from chaos about the middle of the nineteenth century and reappeared in themselves in the form of High Churchism and Ritualism. And this, I think, is rather an extravagant and unwarrantable supposition.

It is hard indeed to conceive how the mere fact of arbitrarily taking up a certain number of doctrines can reach over a dead past of fifteen hundred or at the least a thousand years and connect them with a church that lived only during the three first centuries, or, at the longest, only until the Photian Schism in the ninth century, and that died and was buried then and has lain buried ever since. What proof can they give that the act of reading a new profession of faith, or a mere volition, can restore a dead church to life? By holding any such theory, they virtually claim the credit of having worked a greater miracle than the resurrection of Lazarus.

Lazarus had been only the fourth day in the tomb when, at the bidding of our Divine Lord, he rose to life. Ritualists would have us believe that their forming themselves into a distinct religious body, of which nothing has ever been heard before, has produced the twofold wonderful effect — of bringing back to life a church that had been dead for centuries and of making them, in the very same instant, members of it.

It is in vain, however, that they will strive to stretch over a gulf of fifteen hundred or a thousand years and ask to shake hands with Augustine or Athanasius, Cyril, Ambrose, or Jerome, with the hope they will be recognized by those early heroes of the Faith as members of the same communion.

Were those great Doctors to return again to life, doubtless they would tell them, that while they were willing enough to stretch out to them the hand of charity, yet they could never look upon them as members of the same Church, as long as they did not obey the one central, unfailing authority, from which there was no appeal.

The members of the Ritualistic communion may say that they believe all the Catholic doctrine, and that entering into the Roman Catholic Church would not add anything to their creed except the dogma that teaches that the pope has universal spiritual jurisdiction over the whole earth. I answer that *that* is an essential point. Cardinal Wiseman says:

Never were men more slightly separated from the acknowledged truth than were the Samaritans in the time of our Lord.... Slight as were the dissenting principles of those sectarians, amiable and charitable as may have been their characters, ripe as they were for Christianity, affable and conciliating as the interview (with the Samaritan woman) had hitherto been, no sooner is this important question put, than he makes no allowance, no compromise, but answers clearly and solemnly: "Salvation is of the Jews." ... Thus did this benign and charitable Savior, who came to see and save what was lost, and whose first principle it was: "I will have mercy and not sacrifice"—thus did He hesitate not a moment to pronounce, in the clearest terms, that no deviation from the true religion, however trivial, can be justified or excused in His sight.[39]

The Church of England, then, in all its schools of opinion —High Church, Low Church, Broad Church—with the numberless subdivisions of these great parties, enforces, sanctions, permits, or tolerates the use of the privilege of private judgment in the interpretation of Scripture.

But the use of private judgment in the interpretation of Scripture leads necessarily (taking men as they are) to contradictions in matters of faith and consequently leads necessarily to falsehood in matters of faith.

The very meaning of private judgment as a privilege or principle makes this sufficiently clear. What is its meaning? When

---

[39] Nicholas Patrick Wiseman, *Lectures on the Principal Doctrines and Practices of the Catholic Church*, 3rd ed. (London: Thomas Baker, 1888), pp. 326–328.

analyzed, it plainly means that a number of men, say twenty, may open the Bible, may take any verse of it they like, and may, each of them, give to that verse the interpretation his individual judgment dictates — the meaning that commends itself most to his particular judgment or taste.

Now, men differ in temper of mind, in intellect, in disposition, in character, in education, in convictions, prejudices, leanings, inclinations. A hundred contingencies will influence the meaning they give to the verse in question. The inevitable result of this exercise of liberty will be that, in many cases, one man will give to that verse one interpretation; another will give it an interpretation absolutely contradictory; and each of them, thus using the privilege his church so freely allows him, maintains that *his* view of the matter is quite as likely to be correct as that taken by his neighbor, who gives the inspired words a meaning totally opposite.

And really, looking at the thing from *his* standpoint, it is hard to blame him. For if inspiration, as his Church represents, is abundantly vouchsafed to individuals, he cannot see why *he* may not claim as large a measure of it as his friend, whose life, as far as he can perceive, is not more edifying than his own. Enjoying this fullness of unrestricted freedom, there is nothing to prevent them from differing on every single verse from Genesis to Revelation. And what is more, there is no guarantee that they will agree even in their interpretation of those passages that have reference to the most vital doctrines of Christianity. There is no magisterial authority to bring their minds into oneness of thought.

They recognize no superior control that can adjust their differences; nor does their Church oblige them to recognize any. For, in the twentieth article in which it is stated that she has authority in matters of controversy, in the very same clause, it is implied that she is fallible and quite as liable to err as the least individual who belongs to her communion. Nay, it is implied that the individual has a right to sit in judgment upon her, and to decide whether she ordains anything contrary to God's Word written, or whether she expounds one verse of Scripture so as to be repugnant to another.

She herself does not claim to have a definitive voice; nor does she point to any higher or supreme tribunal from which there is no appeal. Her children are left free to believe that she may go as deeply into error in the interpretation of the Scriptures as the most ignorant and least instructed among them. She may refer them in their controversies to the king as her head or to the Privy Council as the organ of her voice, but in her doing so the hopes of obtaining certainty do not become greater. It is one fallible individual appealing to another equally fallible, or to a tribunal consisting of fallible individuals, all of whom, collectively, admit that their united decision may be as far away from the truth as if it was given separately and individually by each, when a thousand miles away from his fellow councilor.

It is of no use to say that the highest court of appeal in the Church of England never erects itself into a standard with regard to matters of faith or presumes to decide on such matters — that it appeals to the received formularies of the Anglican church and that the most it does is to decide whether some disputed doctrine is opposed to, or is in accordance with, those formularies.

Even so, it formally and authentically interprets them; and, while doing so, admits, at least implicitly, that the interpretation may be wrong, since it does not claim to be infallible — nay, admits that the very articles themselves may be full of error, since they were drawn up by fallible men, men who never claimed, professed, or pretended to be *infallible*.

For, after all, *what are these formularies?* Which is this standard itself, to which all in the Anglican communion, High, Low, and Broad, must bow? What but the teachings and decisions of the English Protestant Reformers of the sixteenth and seventeenth centuries, who can claim no more gift of inerrancy, or an effusion of the Holy Spirit, than the divines of the nineteenth century: fallible men who severed themselves from the traditional teaching of their forefathers and from communion with Rome.

It is hard to discover any theological or solid reason why the dicta of fallible men, who lived three centuries ago, should continue to be the fixed standard of doctrine for Anglicans in the present century.

With such unlimited liberty, then, as the Church of England allows, in sanctioning the use of private judgment, there may be as many contradictory meanings of Scripture as there are individuals who can read its pages, and consequently as many contradictory creeds.

Such is private judgment.

Such it is, such it has been, such it ever *must be*, and such the fatal consequences to which it must necessarily lead. Whether it is gilded by the softer and more refined names of free inquiry, individual preference, liberty of opinion, or freedom of thought, the meaning is the same, and the same inevitable results follow from its application. The use, therefore, of private judgment in the interpretation of Scripture necessarily leads to contradictions in matters of faith, and to contradictions in matters of faith of the most momentous importance.

Let us look at the thing in practice. See what is going on around us. The High Churchman takes out of a certain passage in the New Testament the doctrine that Christ is truly and objectively present in the Eucharist; the Low Churchman interprets the same passage to mean nothing more than a figurative and indefinite presence of our Lord in that mystery, through the faith of the receiver. The Ritualist holds that the words of our Lord recorded in the twentieth chapter of St. John's Gospel, "Receive ye the Holy Spirit"[40] and other such passages prove clearly the power to absolve from sin; his Protestant coreligionist, who has not advanced so far on the road of change and who still clings to the vague doctrines of Low Churchism, loudly asserts that our Lord's words do not prove that power.

Now, surely if any questions of doctrine, in the sphere of religion, ought to be regarded as supremely important in the eyes of man, these ought. No questions in life can be more closely connected with the sanctification and the ultimate salvation of man's soul than the true worship of God, and the right use of Christ's ordinances. And yet, on these most vital points, men who profess to belong to the same church and who fill her highest offices, using their right of private judgment, give absolutely contradictory interpretations to the passages of Scripture that have reference to them.

Hence the almost measureless doctrinal differences that separate the various parties of which that church is now composed. Some with firm conviction believe the Catholic doctrine of the Real Presence; others reject it as intolerable idolatry. Some proclaim their belief in sacramental absolution and express their astonishment that they could have lived so long and read the Scriptures so often without believing it; others repudiate it with horror and disgust and designate it as the pest of society.

Now, I ask, has the church that sanctions a principle that necessarily leads to such interminable contradictions, and, therefore,

[40] John 20:22.

to interminable error, any right to be considered the one true Church of Christ? Can any reasonable man who seriously thinks on the matter hold that Christ meant to leave to His Church the free use of a principle, prerogative, or privilege that would reduce His religion to a Babel of contradictory opinions?

Should anyone hold this, he must be prepared to accept the necessary logical conclusion, which is this: that when Christ gave His Apostles the great commission to preach His gospel to the nations, He authorized Peter to preach the doctrine of the Real Presence in Antioch, authorized John to preach the contradictory in Ephesus, authorized James to preach both the one and the other in Jerusalem — nay, left each Apostle free to affirm that dogma emphatically, and to deny it quite as emphatically, while preaching the very same sermon to the very same audience. And these are conclusions from which these very advocates of private judgment must shrink with horror, if they have any regard for consistency and truth.

If, then, unity is an essential mark of the one true Church of Christ, the Church of England, in her various sections, must give up all claim to divine institution. For unity she has *not*, has never had, and never *can* have. If unity of doctrine were not something entirely beyond her control, why should there have been in the past, and why should there be in the present, so many different parties holding opposite opinions on the most momentous matters of revelation; with all of them, we must remember, tolerated, and mutually tolerating one another, as recognized parties in the same communion; with each and all claiming a common right to hold their place, as representing the varied multiform views of one and the same comprehensive Anglican church?

But she does not profess to have it.

Unity

So far from having any principle that can be a bond, a guarantee, a preservative, a protection of unity, she asserts a principle that makes unity an impossibility. And the history of her variations in the past, her present actual state, the numberless divisions into which she has been torn, are striking illustrations of the disintegrating power of her principle.

All these things furnish tangible and irresistible proof that identity of doctrine can never live side by side with the unrestricted use of the privilege of free inquiry. Let us take some facts from history. Protestantism was not seventy years old when it was divided into 270 sects. Staphylus and Cardinal Hosius counted 270 branches of it before the end of the sixteenth century.[41]

Calvin, secretly lamenting the wreck the Reformation had made of Christian unity, wrote to Melanchthon that he was anxious to hide, as far as possible, the hideous spectacle of their interminable divisions from the gaze of the world, and particularly from the eyes of future generations.[42] "It is of great importance," he says, "that the divisions which subsist among us should not be known to future ages; for nothing can be more ridiculous than that we, who have been compelled to make a separation from the whole world, should have agreed so ill among ourselves from the very beginning of the Reformation."[43]

---

[41] Friedrich Staphylus (1512–1564) was a German theologian, at first a Protestant and then a Catholic convert. Stanislaus Hosius (1504–1579) was a Polish Roman Catholic cardinal.

[42] John Calvin (1509–1564) was a leading French theologian and pastor during the Protestant Reformation. Philip Melanchthon (1497–1560) was a German reformer and a collaborator with Martin Luther.

[43] Jean Calvin and Jules Bonnet, *Letters of John Calvin*, vol. 2 (New York: B. Franklin, 1973), 376–377.

Beza wrote to Dudith in the same tone: "Our people," he says, "are carried away by every wind of doctrine. If you know what their religion is today, you cannot tell what it may be tomorrow. In what single point are those Churches, which declared war against the Pope, united among themselves? There is not one point which is not held by some of them as an article of faith and by others rejected as an impiety."[44]

Melanchthon was quite as loud in his lamentation over the Babel of discordant creeds generated by the doctrines of the Reformers as either of the two whom I have quoted: "The Elbe," he says, "with all its waters, could not furnish tears enough to weep over the miseries of the distracted Reformation."[45]

The character, nature, and principle of private judgment is to produce variety and difference of opinion, and even civil and general war. How great and multiform that variety is — how wide that difference — is abundantly demonstrated in *Whitaker's Almanac* this very year! In it, we find that places for religious worship in England and Wales have been certified to the Registrar General on behalf of more than 220 sects. The list is alphabetical; it begins with the Advent Christians and ends with the Young Women's Christian Association: very nearly all these sects have had their origin in the errors of the Reformation.

But why use further arguments in words? Is not the logic of facts sufficient to prove the point? Look at the Church of England

---

[44] Théodore de Bèza, *Epistles*, Epist. ad Aud. Dudit. Théodore Bèza (1519–1605) was a French Protestant Christian theologian and a disciple of John Calvin. Andreas Dudith (1533–1589) was a Hungarian nobleman, bishop, humanist, and diplomat in the Kingdom of Hungary.

[45] Bèza, *Epistles* 2, 202.

in her present actual state. Some of those who subscribe to her articles profess all the doctrines taught by the Catholic Church, except the supreme universal spiritual jurisdiction of the pope over the world. They profess to hold the Real Presence, transubstantiation, sacramental Confession, the Sacrifice of the Mass, Purgatory, the invocation of Mary and of the saints, and nearly all the other doctrines that are contained in the Roman Catholic creed. Others reject all these doctrines as damnable superstition.

Now, by what effort of the mind can these two parties be said to be one? By what process of reasoning can it be established that the Church that allows such contradictions to be professed within her pale is one? On what principle can it be said that she has that unity that is essential to truth? What idea can we have of falsehood if we hold that the Church of England is true — is the one true Church of Christ?

But this want of unity is common not merely to all branches of the Church of England; it is common to all religious bodies outside the Church of Rome. As unity cannot be found in any heretical church, so neither can it be found in any schismatic church.

The Oriental schismatic churches cannot pretend to possess it. They have always been willing to sacrifice unity of creed to "state" expediency. They do not aim, and cannot aim, at anything higher than material or political unity. On the same principle that Photius and Michael Cerularius broke with Rome,[46] and denied the supremacy of the Roman pontiff, so the bishops of those schismatic churches may, either individually

---

[46] Photius I (ca. 810–ca. 893), was the ecumenical patriarch of Constantinople from 858 to 867 and from 877 to 886. Michael I Cerularius (ca. 1000–1059) was the ecumenical patriarch of

Let There Be No Divisions Among You

or collectively, sever their connection with their respective patriarchates, deny entirely the authority of their respective patriarchs, and form themselves into distinct and separate religious bodies.[47]

As a matter of fact, schism has already produced its inevitable consequences in those regions of the East that are still under its sway. It is well known that the Russian Church is undermined throughout her length and breadth by sects that, at the present moment, number the greater part of the population—sects, too, that are filled with the most desperate hatred toward both imperial and patriarchal jurisdictions. There are few who have not heard that the late Czar Nicholas often predicted that Russia would perish by her religious divisions. Now, a Church that is torn by increasing and incurable schisms can hardly have the boldness to pretend that a necessary, unfailing bond of unity is one of her essential characteristics.

But now, which *alone* among all the churches has this mark of unity? Cardinal Wiseman gives the answer. He says there is one simple way of demonstrating which church has the right to claim it: by showing which is the Church that *alone actually*

Constantinople from 1043 to 1059, famed for his mutual excommunication with Pope Leo IX that led to the Great Schism.

[47] It may be said that the Greek church is very tenacious of Catholic doctrines and Catholic traditions. I answer: the Greek church cannot continue to have unity of faith, for as all-important controversies on questions of faith have arisen in every age in the past, so all-important questions of a similar kind will arise again; and, on the other hand, she has no infallible *"judex controversiarum,"* i.e., no infallible judge of controversies, either in a pope or in a general council to appeal to, who could settle such matters definitively.

claims it. He adds that if we find that all other churches give up their right and title to it, it follows that they can have no pretension to it; and if only one church assumes it as one of its characteristics, assuredly we have enough to prove that it alone possesses it. "With regard to unity," he observes:

> all say that they believe in one Church, and profess that the true Church can be only one. But the Catholic Church is the only one which requires absolute unity of faith among all its members; not only so, but—as by principles alone I wish to try the question—the Catholic Church is the only one that holds a principle of faith essentially supposing unity as the most necessary quality of the Church. The Catholic Church lays down, as its principle and ground of faith, that all mankind must believe whatever she decides and sanctions, with the assistance of the Holy Spirit; and this is a principle necessarily directed to bring all men's minds into oneness of thought. Its essence, therefore—its very soul—that which gives it individuality—is the principle of unity.
>
> The principle of the others is that each individual must judge for himself and make out his own system of faith: now dispersion, dissension, and variety are necessarily the very essence of a Church which adopts that principle. And this, in fact, is practically demonstrated. For the character, nature, and principle of private judgment is to produce variety and difference of opinion, and even civil and general war. Thus clearly in the Catholic Church alone does the principle of unity exist.[48]

[48] Wiseman, *Lectures on the Principal Doctrines*, lect. 9, pp. 271–272.

Let There Be No Divisions Among You

Yes, the Catholic Church, and the Catholic Church alone, can claim this essential mark of truth, for she alone actually possesses it. Her mode of teaching excludes absolutely every principle, prerogative, or privilege that could lead to contradiction in the domain of doctrine. She interdicts the use of private judgment in matters of faith now, she has ever interdicted it, and she will continue to interdict it to the end of time. Free inquiry, individual preference, liberty of mind, freedom of thought, private judgment, in the domain of faith are words that she has no ears to hear.

She will not, she cannot, listen to them. They would rend the rock on which she rests.

She takes her stand on the unchanging truths of Him who built her; and she will tolerate no human pretensions that would tend to split them asunder. Nor will she suffer any sophistry, however plausible, that would generate the least deviation from them. Her teaching is one, absolute, clear, unerring, emphatic, definitive.

No creeds of human origin can rear their heads within her pale, except to be branded with her loud and withering anathemas. She will never recognize any appeal from her tribunal. She will suffer none of her children to sit in judgment upon her decrees. In all places, at all times, in all circumstances, her voice is unchanging.

High position, boundless wealth, literary attainments, vast erudition, transcendent ability, genius even of the highest order, make no difference. With the king and the subject, the philosopher and the savage, the rich and the poor, the young and the old, her method of teaching is the same. To the youth of fifteen and the old man of fourscore she speaks in the same tone.

To each generation of her children, as they grow up to an age to understand her symbol of faith, she says with the authoritative voice of her Founder:

Unity

You are but of yesterday; you are but fifteen, twenty, thirty, fifty, eighty, at most a hundred years of age. *You* did not live in the days of Jesus Christ to hear the doctrines He commanded to be believed and the precepts He commanded to be fulfilled. But *I* lived in His time, for *I* am His Church, His spouse. And I have brought down in my bosom through the centuries that have since rolled away the doctrines He revealed to the world and the sense in which He meant them to be received—the precepts He imposed and the manner in which He meant them to be fulfilled. It is *mine* to teach you. It is *yours* to listen and to believe. But it is *not* yours, and it never *can* be yours, to build up a creed out of your own head.

This mode of teaching bears upon it the impress of divine institution. Here is a bond of unity. Here is a bulwark of unity. Here is unity in principle and unity in practice—and unity in word and unity in meaning. Neither practical error nor speculative error, neither rationalism, nor indifferentism, nor liberalism, nor latitudinarianism, nor agnosticism, nor any other religious system of human invention, can ever find a shelter in this impregnable citadel of God's one, perfect, unchanging, everlasting truth.

Chapter 8

∞

Universality

What is meant by universality as an essential mark of the one true Church of Christ? It is well to define our meaning, for wrong impressions may easily be formed. Universality, or catholicity,[49] in the sense in which it is an essential mark of the one true Church, is nothing else but such extension as to time, territorial space, number of members, as will make it clear to all who choose to inquire that she is the only Church among all religious bodies in which is found a permanent unity of faith springing from a necessary unfailing principle of faith; and therefore the only one that can justly claim to be the Church instituted by Christ.

Hence, when we hold that she must have universality as an essential note of her truth, we do not mean that she must necessarily exist in every country of the globe, from pole to pole, simultaneously. Nor do we mean that she must have at all times, or at any time, the greater part of the human race enrolled as members of her fold. Nor do we mean that in every period of her

---

[49] In the words of the *Maynooth Catechism*: "The Church is catholic or universal, because she has subsisted in every age, is spread through all nations, and shall last to the end of time."

history, or in any period of it, it must be clear that in point of numbers she is far ahead of the various heretical and schismatic sects taken collectively. Nor do we mean even that her members must necessarily be more numerous than some individual heresy or schism, which, for the hour, has become particularly rampant and particularly popular.

No. Numbers however great, space however wide, duration however long, none of these things singly, nor all of them collectively, can constitute universality in the sense in which it is a necessary note of the one true Church.

Universality is rather the transparent medium through which her unity becomes strikingly visible. For it is, we may say, the unity of the Church illustrated and manifested in a sufficiently large and wide sphere, to make that unity a visible, striking, unmistakable proof of truth. *Such* unity, producing oneness of thought on so large a scale, holding permanently so many people of different times, of different climes, different tongues, different character, in one and the same faith, is something that cannot be accounted for on merely natural grounds, and consequently presupposes the divine institution of the thing to which it belongs.

Hence, that the Church of Christ be universal, in the sense in which universality is a mark of her truth, it is not necessary that she should be simultaneously and mathematically universal. Her action on the nations of the world is not to be measured by mathematical dimensions: majority of numbers and vastness of territory do not constitute this mark.

It is not impossible that God, whose wise providence rules all things, might allow one nation after another to lose the Faith, as punishment of the abuse of grace — might permit persecution so to cripple her power and thin her children that her sphere would be narrowed to within a very much smaller space than that which she now occupies. He might allow liberalism, agnosticism, or atheism to wrench from her bosom as many members as she lost in the great apostasy of the sixteenth century, without her acquiring any New World, where millions of conversions would compensate her for her loss. Such diminution of her numbers, however—such narrowing of her sphere—would not deprive her of that universality that is an essential mark of truth.

However small the numbers to which apostasy might reduce her—however narrow the limits within which persecution might confine her, there would still shine on her brow the star that would make it clear that she was the Church of all times and of all nations—her identity with the Church of the centuries and generations of the past would be clearly discernible; and she would continue ever to be the Church, of which alone it could be said that she, and she only, had the potentiality of universality—that is, a power that would make her even absolutely universal, if the passions, prejudices, and obstinacy of men did not prevent her from doing so.

Now, it is on this potentiality, power, or capacity of universality that I wish chiefly to ground my argument. Although the members of the Church in communion with Rome reach a higher figure than is reached by the members of all other Christian bodies taken collectively, yet I will not take advantage of this majority of numbers. Numbers ebb and flow. The crops of the earth in some particular year may be fourfold what they were the year before, and tenfold what they are the year following. Universal war and widespread epidemic may reduce the population of the earth by many millions in a decade.

No, I will take ground that cannot be disputed, for it is my settled purpose not to draw any inference except from premises that will be easily granted or at least can admit of being proved. I will argue from that inborn property or power of universality that is essential to the very existence of the Church of Christ and of which visible universality is nothing but the external manifestation. This is the point on which I wish to insist most.

Whichever church is Christ's was His Church before she became actually universal in any sense. She *could* and *did* exist before she was widely spread.

She was as truly His Church while she was still confined within the walls of Jerusalem as when some centuries later she had reduced the East and the West under her sway and counted her members in millions. But she never *was* His Church, and she never *could be* His Church, without having the innate potentiality of universality. This inherent power of making herself universal, as far as people will allow her to become universal, is essential to her being. It was implanted in her on the day of Pentecost, when she stepped forth in all her completeness from the hands of her Founder and when His Divine Spirit descended into her to dwell in her forever. And the vast space she was afterward to cover and the millions of members she was afterward to count in the course of her long and glorious history were to be but the visible results of that power in action.

I have said: whichever church is Christ's must be one that has the potentiality of universality. This statement is easily proved.

As Christ died for all, He instituted His Church for the salvation of all, since He meant His Church to be instrumental in saving all whom He died to redeem.

The salvation of the whole human race was the sole object He had in view when He founded her on the everlasting rock and when He gave His Apostles the great commission to bear her message of faith to all the nations of the earth. And it was that she might be instrumental in saving the human race, not merely in one stage of its career, but in all its generations to the end of time, that He promised to remain with her all days, down to the consummation. In other words, He did not bring her into life that she might save the people of Asia only, or of Africa only, or of Europe only, or of Ireland, England, or Scotland only, but that she might save the people of all countries and of all centuries.

His intention and desire in founding her covered exactly the same space and the same duration as was covered by His intention and desire in working out Redemption. As His Redemption was to take in the people of all places and of all ages, so did He mean His Church to embrace, within her bosom, mankind of every place and of every time. If He redeemed all, it was that all might be saved; if He instituted His Church, it was that all might be saved by her, for through her He meant the fruits of His copious and universal Redemption to be communicated to all for whom He shed His blood and gave His life.

No one can deny that such were His intentions.

That some, that many men in every age were to refuse to listen to her voice, were to shut their eyes to her signs, to persecute, to imprison, to murder those who sought to bring to them her saving message, does not interfere with His merciful and loving designs. As His blood was to be shed for many in vain, so His Church would be founded for many in vain—both for many within her and for many without her, who would persistently refuse her proffered graces.

Let it be borne in mind that as yet I am not saying which Church has this essential mark of truth. My contention at present is that Christ meant His Church for the salvation of the people of *all* nations and of *all* times.

But if He meant her to save all, He must have meant her to *reach* all, as far at least as people would allow themselves to be reached by her. In other words, He must have so constructed her that she should have the potentiality or power of making herself even absolutely universal, unless the malice, blindness, obstinacy, passions, or prejudices of men prevented her from doing so. More than this, He must have meant her to be continually striving throughout all time to enlarge her sphere—to make her light shine more and more widely—to bring her gospel of truth to those who had it not. All reasonable Christians will admit that any church that does not fit in this frame can have no claim to be considered the one true Church of Christ.

Now here, quite independently of any argument taken from comparison of numbers—quite independently of any argument taken from the relative success of the efforts made by the various Christian denominations to convert the heathen—quite independently too of any argument taken from the names of those churches or sects whose names indicate their geographical boundaries and mark them out as national or local institutions—quite independently of all this, we have ground enough to show that the Church of England has not this essential mark of the one true Church of Christ. *Not only does she not have it, but she cannot by possibility ever have it.*

No church that does not have unity of faith, springing from a necessary, unfailing principle conservative of that unity, can ever possibly have the potentiality of universality; and, therefore, can never possibly have the mark of universality, since the mark is but the outgrowth of the innate power. As long as it has not a bond to keep it united as one and the same thing, it can never have in itself the germ of universal growth. Its inherent elements of discord will prevent it from multiplying in its original form.

Universality

An army, in point of overwhelming numbers, perfect discipline, complete equipment, skill of commander, invincible courage on the part of its officers and of its rank and file, may be, in the opinion of the most competent judges, more than strong enough to subdue all the nations of the earth. It has hardly begun, however, its work of universal conquest, when discord becomes visible in its ranks. It is split into two opposite camps that fight against each other and continue to fight against each other. Reconciliation is hopeless. The elements of division spread, and break up the two great sections into minor opposing bands, until every trace of union has disappeared.

It is clear that such an army, however numerous, however brave, however well armed and well officered, can never reduce the world under one scepter: actual division makes that impossible. In like manner, some new religion appears. It panders to men's prejudices, flatters men's passions, professes to impose some semblance of restraint, while it leaves them comparatively free both as to faith and to morals. It is easily made plausible through the ingenious rhetoric of its propagandists. It quickly becomes popular with the multitude; it may make proselytes in thousands in the hour of wild, unreasoning excitement; it may even bring some nations under its sway for the time. But having within itself the elements of division, being devoid of that union that constitutes at once strength and individuality, having no bond of cohesion to keep it together as one united whole, it will be rent inevitably into different sects before it gets half across the world, and so will fail utterly to reduce mankind under one symbol of faith.

Hence, no church that has not an unfailing, necessary principle of unity can ever possibly have the potentiality or mark of universality. Even granting it facilities, which can never be realized in practice, its teaching can never by any possibility spread universally.

Remove all impediments, put away all opposition springing from the blindness, obstinacy, malice, passions or prejudices of men, let all the nations of the earth be cheerfully willing to listen to and to embrace its teaching, let every circumstance of time and place favor its apostolate; and withal, it cannot possibly ever have the mark of universality, since it does not possess the inborn power from which universality springs. It will teach one nation one set of doctrines, and another nation their corresponding contradictories; or, perhaps, it will teach one and the same nation a hundred distinctly different doctrines.

We have not far to go to find a practical illustration of this. Look at the Church of England, within the very shores from which she takes her name. Can she be said to have kept her members in the same belief even in that very territory within which she is dominant? Certainly not. In the very realm where the religion she teaches is the established one, where she is helped, subsidized, encouraged, stimulated by the machinery of the greatest civil power the sun ever shone upon, she has not succeeded in keeping her members in the same creed, except in the broad sense of a widespread, universal, multiform, antagonism to the Church of Rome. She may indeed have the mark of universality in that sense.

But to say that England ever did profess, or is professing now, Protestantism as one united, uniform creed, would be as great an error as to assert that England, France, Germany, Austria, Russia, Turkey, China, and North and South America were united under one and the same crowned head.

Those who profess her religion at the present moment are not under her control, either as to doctrines of faith or precepts of morality. *She* is entirely under *their* control. They circumscribe her boundaries, define her sphere, mark out her work, sit in judgment upon her, frequently take the punishment of clergymen into their own hands, make decrees for the regulation of her worship, and change them at their pleasure.

To this fact—the fact that in her are found the elements of inevitable discord, interminable contradiction, endless division—her notorious want of success in her attempts to evangelize the people of pagan lands is to be ascribed. The average pagan, though not deeply read, though not skilled in close reasoning, has nevertheless sense enough to perceive that there cannot be much truth in a religion in which there are so many opposite opinions. Some of them, after hearing contradictory expositions of faith from the lips of those sectarian missionaries who sought to Christianize them, have been heard to say that Christians seemed to have as many different religions as paganism had gods. "There is no greater barrier," says Mr. Colledge, a Protestant British official in China, "to the spread of the Gospel of our Savior among the heathen than the division and splitting which have taken place among the various orders of Christians themselves.... Let us ask any intelligent Chinese what he thinks of this, and he will tell us that these persons cannot be influenced by the same great principle, but that Europe and America must have as many Christs as China has gods."[50]

A Church that has not a bond of unity proceeding from an unfailing principle of unity can never become universal. A thing

---

[50] T.R. Colledge, Esq., "Suggestions with Regard to Employing Medical Practitioners as Missionaries to China," *Chinese Repository* 9 (1836): 389.

that has not permanent identity can never possess the power or quality of universal assimilation.

The Church of England has no bond of unity and therefore can never possibly have that mark or capacity of universality that is essential to the one true Church of Christ. The Church of Rome, as we have seen, is the only one that possesses such a bond of unity, and hence she alone can ever possibly realize universality in practice.

∞

This potentiality of universality must be one that slumbers not: it must be ever active and energizing. Whichever Church is Christ's must be one of which impartial history can testify, that she has been striving actively and energetically ever from her first beginnings and throughout her whole career to propagate her Faith more and more widely through pagan lands. Any Church that has not exhibited at all times, when there was any opportunity of doing so, this characteristic of active zeal for the conversion of the heathen cannot have any claim to be considered the one true Church of Christ. If there be any persons who have any difficulty in granting this, a few words will make the matter clear.

The sun cannot be in the heavens above us without sending forth rays of light. There may be an eclipse, there may be a mist black as night, but still, from the very fact that he is in the sky, he must send forth his beams, and those beams must reach us, unless some accidental cause darkens the medium through which they are meant to be conveyed to us.

The Church was designed by Christ, her Founder, to be the light of the world, and to be the light of the world of every century and of every generation.

He Himself who is the Eternal Sun of Justice and who styled Himself the Light of the World, promised to be in her all days, that she might be such. He meant her light to shine upon the people of all times and of all places. Consequently, His desire to dispel the darkness of paganism did not end with the death of His first Apostles. When He gave them the commission to teach all nations, He foresaw that the martyr's death would overtake them before they had succeeded in making His gospel known to all nations.

He could not mean that as soon as the grave had closed over their remains, His Church was to cease entirely the work of propagating the Faith and was thenceforward to make no further effort to make her light shine in those regions that were still in the darkness of idolatry and in the shadow of death.

We cannot hold that such was His design without being forced to the conclusion that, while He had at heart the salvation of those who lived in the days of His first Apostles, He had no concern as to what became of the pagan nations of the second, third, and fourth centuries, and of every century to the end of time.

It is clear that He meant her to continue throughout all ages her efforts to evangelize the nations to spread her light farther and farther over the earth; else she would fail to fulfill the end for which He founded her.

It is clear also that if He promised to be with His first Apostles by a special presence of His power and guidance, in order to stimulate and help them to do the work of propagating His Faith everywhere, He meant that promised presence to extend to their successors throughout all generations. And this for the simple reason, that the dissipation of the darkness of idolatry, and the replacing of it by the light of His gospel, were works that would be as dear to His Sacred Heart throughout all time, as they were on the memorable day when He spoke the words: "Going, teach all nations."

Since, then, Christ has dwelt permanently in His Church, since He is the light of the world, since He must have at all times a constant, active, efficacious desire that His light should illuminate the whole earth, it follows that His Church must be one, of which the unprejudiced historian can relate that, during her whole career, she, above all others, has manifested a strong impulse — a necessarily active desire to bring heathen nations within her communion.

But which among all the Churches now existing can honestly claim from the impartial records of the past this glorious testimony? Can the Anglican church, the Lutheran church, or the Calvinist church lay any claim thereto?

No. They did not begin to exist until toward the middle of the sixteenth century, and consequently could not have evangelized the peoples of the long centuries that had passed away before they were born. And even for the few years of their comparatively short career, they cannot stand the application of this test. For they had been a considerable period in existence before they showed any inclination at all to make the light of their creed shine on the idolater.

Besides, this was not their scope. Their sphere was meant to be purely local. Their original framing excluded all idea of organization for wide foreign missionary enterprise — in fact, for missionary enterprise of any kind. They were to be but a part of the state in which they were to subsist. They were to be under state control and consequently were to partake of the nature of the constitution whose established religion they were to be. And a religion formed to suit the taste of some particular nation is not likely ever to become a religion of universal adoption. A religion that suits the government of one country may not suit the government of another country and is certain not to suit the government of every country.

At all events, being created and kept in life by an act of Parliament, they could not make any move to convert the heathen, unless directed, encouraged, helped, and subsidized by the state whose dominant religion they represented. And surely we cannot say that Christ ever meant His Church, which He founded to evangelize all the nations of the earth, to be directed in the measure and exercise of her zeal for the salvation of souls, by the laws of any particular country, and to be guided in her efforts for the propagation of the Faith in pagan lands, according to the dictates of any particular civil power.

That I am not making groundless statements, or putting the thing in a false light, will be evident from the following testimonies, which undoubtedly cannot be said to be taken from prejudiced sources.

Lord Macaulay, whose opposition to the Catholic Church is sufficiently known to make it certain that he does not say anything in her praise except what he believes to be true, draws a contrast between her action and that of the Reformed churches in the seventeenth and eighteenth centuries. In any case, the truth of his statement is patent to all. He says:

> As the Catholics in zeal and union had a great advantage over the Protestants, so had they an infinitely superior organization. In truth, Protestantism, for aggressive purposes, had no organization at all. The Reformed Churches were mere national Churches. The Church of England existed for England alone. It was an institution as purely local as the Court of Common Pleas, and was utterly without

machinery for foreign operations. The Church of Scotland, in like manner, existed for Scotland alone. The operations of the Catholic Church took in the whole world.[51]

For about two centuries and a half—that is, from her institution until the beginning of this century—Protestantism confined her zeal within those dominions to which she owes her creation and to which she owes the continuance of her life. During the whole of that long period she manifested no compassion, no consideration for the poor idolater.

She let him go his way, and left him to perish helplessly in his darkness, without making any attempt to stretch out to him the hand of relief, although the constantly increasing commerce of the great empire that she represented gave her every facility for doing so. She remained satisfied with her work at home, enjoyed her repose with dignity, and went on sleeping the sleep of undisturbed peace. Then suddenly, in the beginning of this century (about the year 1805), she awoke from her slumber, shook off her drowsiness, became alive to a sense of her culpable apathy, and seemed anxious to make a great, a vigorous, a stupendous effort for the propagation of the Faith—such an effort as would make amends for long and grave neglect. Enormous sums of money for evangelizing purposes were produced; missionaries were sent out in thousands to pagan lands; millions of Bibles and numberless tracts were distributed in pagan towns—that is, in pagan ports and all along the coasts.

---

[51] Review of Leopold Ranke's *The Ecclesiastical and Political History of the Popes of Rome during the Sixteenth and Seventeenth Centuries*, in Thomas Babington Macaulay, *Critical, Historical, and Miscellaneous Essays and Poems*, vol. 3 (Philadelphia: Porter and Coates, 1879), 486.

It is evident, then, that neither past nor contemporary history can bear testimony that she has been throughout her career the evangelizing Church of the nations.

But now comes the question: Can the Greek schismatic churches claim to have evangelized perpetually?

No. They have never pretended or professed to be missionary churches at all. They are mere national churches—purely local institutions like the Church of England; but *unlike* the Church of England, they have made no attempt even in this nineteenth century to convert the heathen. As to the Greek-Russian Church, it not only fails to convert the heathen tribes subject to the empire, but does not always even wish to do so.

Hence the Greek schismatic churches do not and cannot ask to claim from history the testimony that they have been striving assiduously, throughout their course, to make the light of Christianity shine in heathen lands.

One Church, and one Church alone, can claim this glorious testimony.

Need I say it is the Church of Rome?

She has been the great evangelist of the nations throughout all time since the days of the Apostles. If it be asked, who gave to England that Christianity whose form was changed and mutilated at the Reformation, Venerable Bede answers the question to the satisfaction of all. Speaking of England's conversion, he says: "And whereas he [Pope Gregory] bore the pontifical power all over the world, and was placed over the churches already reduced to the faith, he made our nation, till then given up to idols, the Church of Christ."[52]

[52] Bede, *The Ecclesiastical History of the English Nation*, vol. 1 (London: James Bohn, 1845), 68.

Let There Be No Divisions Among You

Who gave to Germany the religion that she abolished in the revolt of Luther? Do not all impartial records show that it came from missionaries who had with them the approval, the credentials, and the blessing of the Roman pontiff?

Dr. Milman, some years ago dean of St. Paul's, in his *History of Latin Christianity*, after showing that one nation after another received the gospel through the voice of the Church of Rome, adds:

> All these conquests of Christianity were in a certain sense the conquests of the Roman See.... Reverence for Rome penetrated with the Gospel to the remotest parts. Germany was converted to Latin Christianity. Rome was the source, the center, the regulating authority recognized by the English apostles to the Teutons. The clergy were constantly visiting Rome as the religious capital of the world ... and bishops from the remotest parts of the empire, and of regions never penetrated by the Roman arms, looked to Rome as the parent of their faith if not to an infallible authority, at least to the highest authority in Christendom.[53]

Colonel Mitchell, in his *Life of Wallenstein*, says:

> Deep and indelible is the debt which religion and civilization owe to the early Roman Pontiffs and to the Church of Rome. They strove long and nobly to forward the cause of human improvement, and it is difficult to say what other power could have exercised so beneficial an

[53] Henry Hart Milman, *History of Latin Christianity*, 9 vols. (London: John Murray, 1867), 307.

142

Universality

influence over the fierce and fiery nations which established themselves on the ruins of the Roman empire, after
rooting out all that remained of ancient art and ancient
knowledge. Nor were their efforts confined within those
territorial limits. Monks and missionaries, disregarding
personal danger, penetrated into the forests of Germany
and into the distant regions of the North, and, unap-
palled by the deaths by torture to which so many holy
men had fallen victims, preached to the heathen and
barbarian the mild doctrines of Christianity, which only
sprang up in Europe watered by the blood of saints and
martyrs. Even the efforts of the Church to interpose its
spiritual power in the direction of temporal matters, and
to control the conduct of kings and princes, were benefi-
cial in an age when the clergy alone possessed whatever
learning was extant; and the uniformity of belief which
rendered all the Western Churches dependent on the
Pope, an authority so greatly enlightened, when con-
trasted with the general darkness of the times, became
a principal cause of the progress and prosperity of the
Catholic world.[54]

Such are the testimonies of Protestant writers. Who brought
the light of the Faith to France and made her a Catholic nation?
Missionaries who came in the name and with the authority and
benediction of the See of Rome.

Who evangelized Spain? Who brought to Austria and her
tributaries the Faith she now professes? Who led Ireland and

---

[54] John Mitchell, *The Life of Wallenstein, Duke of Friedland* (London: J. Fraser, 1840), 4–5.

Scotland to a knowledge of the true Gospel? Who gave to the various nations of the East that religion (I mean orthodox religion) that they professed in all its completeness and integrity, until schism rent them from the parent stock? Either the first Apostles who recognized Peter as their head, or their successors who recognized Peter's See—the See of Rome—as the head of all the Churches, and proclaimed union with that See to be a necessary qualification for membership in the one true fold of Christ.

Go through all the countries of Europe, of Asia, of Africa that ever professed the Christian religion in its completeness and perfectness, trace their Christianity to its source, and you will find that source to be none other than the energizing power—the necessarily active, unfailing impulse to evangelize—which is ever found in the Church of which Peter's successor is the visible head.

All impartial records of the past agree in stating the undeniable fact that, from the days of the Apostles down to the present time, the Church of Rome has been constantly, untiringly exerting her power to bring idolatrous nations under the sway of the Gospel of Christ. There is no other Church of which this can be said. She alone, among all the religious bodies that now exist, has manifested throughout her career that sacred energy—that holy, earnest, necessarily active zeal for the conversion of the heathen and the heretic that must ever characterize the Church in which dwells the Savior of souls, who founded her as much for the salvation of the people of the nineteenth century and of every century to the day of doom, as for the salvation of the people who lived in the age that witnessed her institution.

Let the impartial Christian look these facts in the face: let him view them in the light of faith: let him ponder on them with unbiased mind, and he will have no difficulty in deciding which class of missionaries has the stronger claim to be considered the apostles of the Church that was destined in the designs of the Most High to be the Teacher of the nations.

The title of "Catholic," or "Church of the World," has been vindicated nearer home, and not long ago. It has been the privilege of this generation to witness the most striking manifestation of her universality that the world has ever seen. Nothing else could have shown so clearly that only the limits of the world can bound her zeal; that nothing but the confines of the earth can limit her power of expansion; that she alone has a right to be styled the Church of the Universe. I allude to the late Ecumenical Council of the Vatican (1869–1870). It would look as if God, in His wise providence, had reserved this worldwide vindication of her claim for this particular epoch, when the sects have affected to despoil her of it, or to share it with her. We shall not undertake to describe this magnificent scene ourselves; we shall leave the description of it to those outside the fold, who cannot help expressing their involuntary admiration of it.

The hall of assemblage, the number of prelates, the mitered heads, the distant climes from which many of them came, the different tongues they spoke, the antiquity of the heritage they represented, the power of the unbroken unity that had brought them together, their submissive attitude in the presence of the Common Father the Supreme Pontiff, their unanimous submission to his decree: all this was sketched in eloquent and graphic language by the correspondents of several of the great daily papers of London who were in Rome at the time. Alluding to it on December 10, 1869, the *Standard* said:

Let There Be No Divisions Among You

In historic importance, in traditional dignity, in the splendor of associations that gather round its name, no assembly in the world, past or present, can pretend to compare with the great parliament of the Latin Church. The unbroken continuity of the history of that Church, its undeniable and uninterrupted descent from the Church founded by the Apostles, renders this Council the immediate successor and representative, in a sense in which no other council can rival its claims, of the Council of Nicaea, if not of the Council of Jerusalem. Nor is its actual power and consequence unworthy of its traditional heritage. It is the representative assembly, the omnipotent legislature, of a compact, coherent body of Christians, whose number approaches more nearly to two than to one hundred million.

After referring to the attempts made to hinder the council, the correspondent adds:

Nevertheless, all has been in vain, and the dispassionate observer is compelled to confess that the spectacle of so many hundreds of Bishops, coming from the farthest quarters of the globe, at the beck of an old man, powerless in all but spiritual thunderbolts, and one that, occurring in the 19th century, and especially at this period of it, is calculated to strike the believing with pious admiration, and even the incredulous, like ourselves, with irrepressible astonishment.

On December 14, 1869, the *Daily News* said:

It must be admitted that weak as is the temporal power of the Pope, no other prince could have assembled such a body as met today in the council hall of St. Peter's, and no other could have provided them with such a magnificent temple. From the remotest quarters of the globe, from a land that was just heard of when the Council of Trent sat, from a land that was then wholly unknown, from Palestine and Syria, the cradles of Christianity, from Persia, from China, from India, from Africa, from the Western Isles, as well as from the countries washed by the Mediterranean, men of various tongues, of diverse origin, men of great learning and great age, have come together to this famous city in obedience, voluntary and spiritual obedience, to the pastor who claims to be the successor of St. Peter, and the vicegerent of God upon earth.

Such is the testimony even of those who were not of her fold. Well, indeed, might it be said that that scene was one that was calculated to inspire the believing with "pious admiration, and even the incredulous with irrepressible astonishment." For what other Christian denomination in the world could reveal to the eyes of man a representation of universality, or rather a representation of universal unity, to compare with that which forced these words of glowing eulogium from the pen of hostile writers?

The extension and duration of even the oldest and most widely spread of other Churches dwindle into absolute insignificance when viewed side by side with the prestige, the venerable antiquity, the universal diffusion, the limitless dominion of the Church of Rome. No sectarian Church within the British Isles or beyond them can lay any claim to uniform universality in the face of this overpowering, unanswerable fact—a fact that no amount of sophistry can explain away—the fact of a worldwide diffusion of a Church that is the same everywhere from sunrise to sunset, and whose identity with the Church of the Apostles is clearly traceable through all the centuries that have intervened between their day and our own.

This fact alone, in the judgment of all calm, impartial, reasonable, sincere inquirers, ought to be sufficient to show that in her alone has been realized that undivided luminous universality that must ever distinguish the true Church of Christ—a universality that does not require that she should be found in every part of the globe simultaneously, but that does require that in every spot where she is found, she should be one and the same.

I will close my remarks on this note of her truth by a brief allusion to her perpetual, exclusive, inalienable possession of the title "Catholic."

How came she to have sole possession of that title, if any other church deserved it better, if any other deserved it equally well, if any other deserved it at all? That she has verified the title, that is, that she has been the teacher of the nations throughout all time, since the days of the Apostles, we have already shown. That she alone has possessed the title itself from the beginning is evident from history.

I will give only a few citations from the early Fathers. Such citations can be easily found in abundance; but to introduce them at any length would swell this little book beyond the contemplated limits.

In the first century, it is said of St. Polycarp that he used to offer up prayers constantly for the members "of the Catholic Church diffused throughout the world."[55] Three centuries later St. Cyril, one of the greatest Doctors of the Greek Church, and

---

[55] Eusebius, *Ecclesiastical History* 4, 15. St. Polycarp (69–155) was bishop of Smyrna.

Patriarch of Jerusalem, instructed the faithful thus: "Should you come into a city, do not enquire merely for the house of God, for so heretics call their places of meeting; nor yet ask merely for the Church; but say, the Catholic Church, for this is the proper name."[56] In the same century, St. Pacianus, one of the lights of the Latin Church, speaks in exactly the same tone:

> In the time of the Apostles, you will say, no one was called Catholic. Be it so; but when heresies afterwards began, and under different names, attempts were made to disfigure and divide our holy religion, did not the apostolic people require a name, whereby to mark their unity, a proper appellation to distinguish their head? Accidentally entering a populous city, where are Marcionites, Novatians, and others who call themselves Christians, how shall I discover where my own people meet, unless they be called Catholics? I may not know the origin of the name; but what has not failed through so long a time, came not surely from any individual man. It has nothing to say to Marcion, nor Appelles, nor Montanus. No heretic is its author.
>
> Is the authority of apostolic men, of the blessed Cyprian, of so many aged Bishops, so many martyrs and confessors, of little weight? Were not they of sufficient consequence to establish an appellation which they always used. Be not angry, my brother: Christian is my name, Catholic is my surname.[57]

---

[56] Cyril of Jerusalem, *Catechetical Lectures* 18, 26. St. Cyril of Jerusalem (ca. 313–386) was a distinguished theologian of the early Church.

[57] Pacianus, Epistle 1, *ad Sympronian* v–vii. St. Pacianus (ca. 310–391) was bishop of Barcelona.

St. Epiphanius, a writer of the Greek church, relates that, at Alexandria, those schismatics who adhered to Meletius styled their church the "Church of the Martyrs" while the rest retained for theirs the name of the "Catholic Church."[58] But no one has spoken more clearly or more emphatically on the point than St. Augustine. Here are his words:

> It is our duty to hold to the Christian religion, and the communion of that Church which is called Catholic, and is so called, not by us only, but by all its adversaries. For whether they be so disposed or not, in conversing with others they must use the word Catholic or they will not be understood.[59]

He adds:

> Among the many considerations that bind me to the Church is the name of Catholic, which, not without reason, in the midst of so many heresies, this Church alone has so retained, that although all heretics wish to acquire the name, should a stranger ask where the Catholics assemble, the heretics will not dare to point out any of their own places of meeting.[60]

So was it in the days of St. Augustine; so is it now. The test that was used in his time, and that had been used for long years

---

[58] Epiphanius, *Panarion (against Heresies)* 1. St. Epiphanius of Salamis (ca. 315–403) was bishop of Salamis, Cyprus.

[59] Augustine, *On True Religion* 7, 12. St. Augustine of Hippo (354–430), was an early Christian theologian and philosopher, best known for his autobiographical work, *Confessions*.

[60] *Against the Fundamental Epistle of Manichaeus* 4.

before it, holds good even at the present day. Go through the streets of London, Liverpool, Dublin, Belfast, Glasgow, Edinburgh — of any city through the length and breadth of Christendom — ask your way to the nearest Catholic Church, and he whom you ask, whether he be Methodist, Presbyterian, Protestant, or even the most advanced "Romanistic" Ritualist, will never think of directing you to one of his own conventicles, however stately and magnificent the building may be; he will direct you to some church that is known to be in communion with the See of Rome. If he directs you otherwise, he feels that he is going against his conscience, and that he is leading you astray.

Every effort on the part of the sects, both in the past and in the present, to wrest this title from the Church of Rome, to appropriate it, or share it with her, has failed ignominiously. Those Ritualists and High Churchmen who designate themselves, and seek to be called, Catholics, often draw upon themselves the ridicule of other members of the Establishment.

However, what I have said of superiority of numbers, I say also with regard to the possession of the title "Catholic," i.e., I will not take advantage of it. I do not desire to insist at any length upon it. But what I do wish to insist upon chiefly and emphatically, above all and beyond all, is this: the Church of Christ exists somewhere on earth. Wherever she is and whatever she is, she must have the capacity of universal extension. No church that has not the power of universal extension can be the Church of Christ. No Church can ever have the power of universal extension, except a church that has a bond of unity springing from a necessary, unfailing principle of unity. And no Church on earth has, or claims to have, that necessary, unfailing bond of unity except the Roman Catholic Church. Therefore, she alone can be the one true Church of Christ.

In her alone we find fulfilled these words of prophecy that, in the belief not merely of those who profess her creed, but in the belief of almost all who belong to any denomination calling itself Christian, point to the Kingdom or Church of Christ: "All the ends of the earth shall remember, and shall be converted to the Lord, and all the kindred of the Gentiles shall adore in His sight; for the kingdom is the Lord's, and He shall have dominion over the nations."[61] "Ask of me, and I will give thee the Gentiles for thy inheritance, and the uttermost parts of the earth for thy possession."[62] "Of the increase of his government and peace there shall be no end, upon the throne of David, and upon his kingdom, to order it, and to establish it with judgment and with justice, from henceforth and forever."[63] "Upon thy walls, O Jerusalem, I have appointed watchmen all the day and all the night: they shall never hold their peace. You that are mindful of the Lord, hold not your peace."[64] "Thy gates shall be open continually: they shall not be shut day nor night, that the strength of the Gentiles may be brought unto thee, and their kings may be brought."[65] "From the rising of the sun to the going down thereof, my name is great among the Gentiles: and in every place there is sacrifice, and there is offered to my name a clean oblation; for my name is great among the Gentiles, saith the Lord of Hosts."[66]

Eliminate the Church in communion with Rome from history and from the world, and these prophetic utterances never have had, and never can have, a fulfillment.

[61] Ps. 21:28–29 (RSV = Ps. 22:27–28).
[62] Ps. 2:8.
[63] Isa. 9:7.
[64] Isa. 62:6.
[65] Isa. 60:11.
[66] Mal. 1:11.

Universality

∞

Of course, when I say that the Christianity of all the nations of the earth that have ever professed Christianity is traceable to the first Apostles and their disciples, or to the See of Peter, as its source, I am to be understood as speaking of full and perfect Christianity: not of mutilated and corrupted Christianity.

From the beginning there have been corruptions of the Gospel. As there were heretics in the first century, so there have been heretics in every century since. And as heresiarchs had a certain following even in the days of the first Apostles, it is not surprising that the heresiarchs who came later should have a certain following, too.

If there were a few teachers of error in the early Church, while her numbers were still so small, how can we wonder that there were more as her dominion extended, and as her members multiplied? When some went out of her and remained out of her because they were not of her even in her infancy, when she was still confined within comparatively narrow limits and while the first heralds of her Faith were living to guide, guard, and defend her, and to confirm the truth of her teaching by their miracles, we are not to be astonished that others should go out of her in succeeding ages, when the sound of her voice had gone to the ends of the earth and her children had become countless as the sands of the seashore.

On the contrary, we should rather be astonished if such had not been the case. For had no schisms and heresies arisen within her, as time went on, her history would have been entirely different from what the Apostles foretold it was to be. Those Apostles, so far from holding out assurances that the whole people of every nation, without exception, would receive her Gospel, and come within, and remain within, her fold, and that she was never to have any enemies or any rivals and that her course throughout was to be calm, smooth, prosperous, and free from all opposition, predicted things far different. They predicted, in fact, that condition of things that has been realized throughout her whole history.

"I know," says St. Paul, "that after my departure ravenous wolves will enter in among you, not sparing the flock. And of your own selves will arise men speaking perverse things, to draw away disciples after them."[67] And describing the character of heretics of distant times, he says:

> Know also this, that in the last days shall come dangerous times; men shall be lovers of themselves ... stubborn, puffed up ... having the appearance indeed of godliness [that is, of genuine faith] but denying the power thereof.... But evil men and seducers shall grow worse and worse, erring and driving into error.... There shall be a time when they will not endure sound doctrine; but according to their desires they will heap to themselves teachers having itching ears.[68]

To the same Timothy he writes, "Now the spirit manifestly saith that in the last times some shall depart from the faith, giving heed to spirits of error and doctrines of devils, speaking lies in hypocrisy, and having their consciences seared."[69] And to the Corinthians he writes, "For there must be also heresies, that they also, who are approved, may be manifest among you."[70]

[67] Acts 20:29–30.
[68] 2 Tim. 1:1–5, 13; 4:3.
[69] 1 Tim. 4:1–2.
[70] 1 Cor. 11:19.

Universality

The Apostles felt that the aggressive, laborious, unyielding life of the Church in their own day was an index to her history to the end of time. They preached the Faith, used all their powers to spread it. They were opposed by Simonians, Cerinthians, Ebionites, heretics of various kinds who rose up around them on all sides. They condemned those teachers of error in their separate individual warnings to the faithful. They called a council and condemned error again with united voice. They strove to fix the eyes of the Church's children everywhere on these decrees of condemnation.

And having done this, they continued to preach and to work in spreading the Faith farther and farther, with as much zeal and vigor, as if nothing had been done, or were being done, to thwart them in their efforts. In their mind this state of things indicated, symbolized what was to be the state of things in the Church down to the consummation.

They knew that heresies must come; they knew also that those heresies could not prevent the Church from spreading; and they knew moreover that whether those heresies were to assume large proportions or small, were to cover half the earth or to be confined within some corner of it—whether they were to last for centuries, or to form, break, and disappear like a bubble—that all this was quite accidental, that they could never in any case be an argument against her catholicity, no more than the heresies that appeared in their own day were an argument against it.

Looking at things from this apostolic standpoint, we see clearly the truth of the following statements:

1. The fact that the influence of the Novatian heresy in the third century extended from Rome to Scythia, to Asia Minor, to Africa, and to Spain proves nothing against the catholicity of the Church.

Let There Be No Divisions Among You

2. The fact that the Donatists in the fourth century increased so rapidly in numbers and importance that in a short time they had got possession of four hundred episcopal sees and that all Africa for a period seemed to groan under the weight of Donatism proves nothing against the catholicity of the Church.

3. The fact that the followers of Arius converted the Gothic race to Arian Christianity; that they succeeded in inoculating Mesogoths, Visigoths, Ostrogoths, Alani, Suevi, Vandals, and Burgundians with their errors; that they succeeded, too, in spreading those errors through parts of France, Spain, Portugal, and Italy, and that those errors continued to be professed by numerous disciples in some of those countries for nearly a hundred years and in others for nearly two hundred years, proves nothing against the catholicity of the Church.

4. The fact that Nestorius, in the fifth century, went out of the Church, and induced many others to go out of her and to remain out of her; that his heresy was embraced and supported by some of the oldest churches in Christendom; that it secured the protection of Persia; that it spread from Cyprus to China; that it was taken up by Indians, Medes, Huns, and Bactrians; that it enlarged its dominion, and increased in numbers and importance until it possessed twenty-five archbishoprics; that it had a large portion of Asia all to itself; that, according to the opinion of some, its members, united to those of the Monophysite heresy, at one time outnumbered the whole Catholic Church both in the East and the West; that from its principal seat in Chaldea it sent out missioners

who worked with an activity and success that brought not merely many illustrious personages, but even some nations under its sway; that it held its ground in its varying forms for more than eight hundred years; and that during that long period it succeeded in preventing Catholic missioners from interfering much with the countries of which it had taken possession—even all this proves nothing against the catholicity of the Church.

For, in the first place, all this was but a recurrence in later times, and on a wider scale when the Church was larger, of what had taken place even in the first century when she was smaller and when her first Apostles were still living. Nay, it was but a fulfillment of the Apostles' predictions.

Second, our opponents as well as we regard Novatians, Donatists, Arians, and Nestorians as heretics; and hence the imposing numbers and the wide diffusion of these rebellious bodies over the earth could be no proof of the truth of the doctrines which they taught.

But apart from this, we must look at the matter from another point of view. The fact that Novatians, Donatists, Arians, Nestorians, and other heretics worked hard in spreading their errors does not prove that the Church in communion with Rome did not work equally hard in spreading the truth. Their activity is no proof of her inactivity.

And in order that their labors and successes should be an argument against her claim to catholicity, it would be necessary to show that while they, during several centuries, were so energetic, she, during the same centuries, was idle and apathetic—looked on with folded arms, and made no effort either to dissipate their errors or to propagate her own doctrines more widely.

Let There Be No Divisions Among You

Well, then, open history, and it will reveal to you that, while those worldwide heresies rose and arrayed themselves against her, and strove like Antichrists to supplant her, she was constantly at work in pulling down and raising up, in breaking heresy to pieces and in building up the citadel of truth, in calling her bishops from the remotest parts to sit in council, to judge error and to condemn it, in notifying her decrees to the faithful throughout the world, in exerting her power to the utmost to have those decrees observed, and in sending her light to the most distant regions of the earth; and that light shone everywhere except in those lands that shut their eyes against it, or, through the intrigues of heresy, refused to accept it.

Such had been her constant and untiring activity, that in spite of the ceaseless war heresy had waged against her, and in spite of the pagan persecutions that had sought to stamp her out, she had, by the end of the third and the beginning of the fourth century, propagated the Faith — that is, orthodox Christianity — in the West, in Italy, in Proconsular Africa, in Numidia, in Mauritania, and even among the Africans, i.e., the Getuli and the Moors, who inhabited the interior of the country in the gorges and valleys of the Atlas; and in Spain, in Gaul, in upper and lower Germany, along the borders of the Danube, in Norica (the modern Austria), in Vindelicia (the modern Bavaria), and in Rhetia (at present the Tyrol).

That Faith had reached Britain also through Roman colonies that had gone there in the reign of Claudius. On the shores of the Mediterranean, in Thrace, Heminontis, Rhodope, Scythia, and lower Moesia, flourishing churches had been established. In Macedonia, Thessalonica, Philippi, and Berea, the churches that had been founded by the Apostles and their disciples through their unbroken communion with Rome still maintained their first fervor. In Athens, the capital of Greece, and in Byzantium, which was soon to be the capital of the new empire, the Faith had long been propagated.

In the East, that Faith had already spread from Jerusalem (still true to say, from St. Peter as from its source) over all the cities of Palestine, Phoenicia, and Syria. Caesarea, Palestine, Tyre, Sidon, Ptolemais, Berytus, Tripoli, Biblos, Seleucia, Apamea, Hieropolis, Samosata, and Antioch all had their Churches. At an early date, Bozra in Roman Arabia and Edessa in the Osrhoene had received the gospel. In Mesopotamia and Chaldea, the Churches of Amida, Nisibis, Seleucia, and Ctesiphon were celebrated. Asia Minor, which had been evangelized by St. Paul, had its illustrious Sees of Ephesus, Laodicea, Pergamos, Philadelphia, Thyatira, Tarsus, Mopsuesta, Smyrna, Iconium, Myra, Miletus, Antioch of Pisidia, Corinth, Nice, and Chalcedon. Christians, too, were found in multitudes in the isles of Crete, Cyprus, and the Archipelago. Numerous and flourishing churches had been established in Armenia and even in Persia.

Egypt, in which the Faith had been propagated by St. Mark, who founded the Patriarchate of Alexandria, had so advanced that it was able to send to the Council of Nice the Bishops of Naucrates, Phtinontis, Pelusium, Panephysus, Memphis, and Heraclea. The Thebais, which was soon to produce examples of heroic sanctity, had in the third century several episcopal sees, among them Antinoe, Hermopolis, and Lycopolis. In the Pentapolis, of which Ptolemais was the metropolitan see, many bishoprics had been founded.

In the fourth and fifth centuries she continued her work of evangelizing. While Donatism, Arianism, Pelagianism, Nestorianism, and Eutychianism were drawing away multitudes from her ranks and marshaling them under their respective standards against her, she was actively engaged not merely in striving to stay the progress of their errors, in holding provincial councils, national councils, and general councils to condemn them, and in promulgating her anathemas through all parts of the earth; she was also vigorously engaged in spreading her light in those regions where it had not yet shone, or was shining but faintly.

Her conquests now (and they were conquests of great magnitude) extended far beyond the boundaries of the Roman Empire. She spread her Faith still more widely in Persia, although that kingdom was soon to become one of the strongholds of Nestorianism and a little later was to become the prey of Mohammedanism.

She brought within her fold the Iberians, who inhabited a territory between the Black Sea and the Caspian, which is now known as Georgia. The Abyssinians, whose faith was destined to be, at least for a time, firm and durable, and whose metropolitan was to be the bishop of Ethiopia, were added to her triumphs. She succeeded, too, in Christianizing vast districts of India—I mean districts of it where her gospel had not yet reached. Nay, while her general councils were examining, discussing, and condemning the heresies of the East, she was at the same time making numberless conversions in some of the most distant isles of the West. It was during that period that, through the zeal and labors of St. Patrick and his companions, she leveled the altars of the Druids in Ireland, cleared that country of every trace of paganism, and placed its people from shore to shore in possession of that full and perfect and uncorrupted Christianity which they have never lost. And not long after that she sent to Britain under the guidance of Augustine the band of heroic missionaries who were destined to revive in that kingdom the faith of which it had almost been entirely despoiled in the persecution of Diocletian, or the practice of which, at least, had almost entirely ceased there.

Universality

Now, if Donatism, Arianism, Pelagianism, Nestorianism, and Eutychianism, which occupied such vast portions of the globe, which counted such multitudes of disciples, and which exercised such sway for centuries, furnish no argument against the universality of the Church, it is difficult to see how any serious objection against her universality can be taken from the bulk of the Greek schismatic communions of the present day, or from the wide prevalence of Protestantism that has taken possession of so many countries, and that is professed by so many peoples.

The Greek schismatics of the East as well as the Protestants of the West admit that the disciples of these various early religious bodies were heretics, and in admitting this they are virtually admitting that their own bulk and influence, in themselves, go no way either toward proving that they are members of the true Church or toward proving that the claim of the Church of Rome is weakened or affected in any way through their vastness. This ought to be remembered by those to whom Cardinal Newman refers when he says: "Bulk, not symmetry; vastness, not order, are their tests of truth."[71]

But we may go further. The wide diffusion of Nestorianism, of the Greek schism, of the heresy of the Reformation, is no more an argument against the universality of the Catholic Church than is the wide and wonderful spread of Islam; and the sway that Islam had exercised over so many millions for so many ages is no more an argument against that universality than are those numberless pagans who are outside the pale of Christianity altogether. "Corruptions of the Gospel," says Cardinal Newman

---

71 John Henry Newman, *Certain Difficulties Felt by Anglicans in Catholic Teaching Considered*, 5th ed. (1879), 344.

again, "are as necessary and ordinary a phenomenon, taking men as they are, as its rejection." He asks:

> Is misbelief a greater marvel than unbelief? Or do not the same intellectual and moral principles which lead men to accept nothing, lead them also to accept half, of revealed truth? Both effects are simple manifestations of private judgment in the bad sense of the phrase, that is, of the use of one's own reason against the authority of God.[72]

This is strikingly true. Heresy or schism, however widely spread, interferes no more with the universality of the Church than absolute infidelity. From the outset the Church was only one of a number of communions that professed to be Christian. From the days of the Apostles, true belief, misbelief, and unbelief have walked side by side. Among those who had the gospel preached to them, some received it, some mutilated it, some rejected it. In the twenty-eighth chapter of Acts, we find it stated that many came to the lodgings of St. Paul that they might hear from him an account of the new religion; and that he expounded it to them at great length, "testifying to the kingdom of God, and persuading them concerning Jesus, out of the law of Moses and the Prophets, from morning till night." And it is added that a certain number were persuaded and that others were not persuaded. "Some believed the things that were said, but some believed not."[73]

So was it then; so has it been ever since; so is it now; so will it be to the end of time.

The Church's note of universality does not require it to be otherwise; that note is independent of all rejections, mutilations,

---

[72]   Ibid., 348.
[73]   Acts 28:23–24.

or corruptions of her gospel. It does not rest on the condition that in every century she must have exclusive sway over three-fourths of the globe; or that, in every generation, nine out of ten of the world's population must profess her doctrine. It is not to be measured by mathematical lines.

No. What is essential to it is that, wherever she exists, she should be found at all times and in all circumstances to be one and the same.

And that she is found to be. In point of space, Rome, or the See of Peter, is her center, the boundaries of the earth her only circumference. And, in point of identity, she is now what she was in the days of the Apostles, and what she is now she will continue to be to the end of time; for she is the one and only true Church of the unchanged, unchanging, and unchangeable God.

∞

Conclusion

The theory of indifferentism may help much, strange as it may sound to say so, in the search after the true Church. To realize this fully, we must fix our thoughts again for a moment on some of the many inconsistencies, incoherencies, and endless contra-dictions with which that theory is pregnant.

And, first of all, I would draw attention to this: if God is indifferent as to in what sense men receive His revelation, it follows that He is indifferent as to in what sense they receive His Ten Commandments, since the Ten Commandments are but a portion of His revelation.

Now, I assume that no one who pretends to be a Christian will hold that men are free as the standard of their morality to choose the contradictories of the Commandments. On what grounds, then, can it be affirmed that they are free to choose as the object of their faith the contradictories of His revealed doctrines? Where is the reason for making any difference? Does not such a system do away with the distinction between truth and falsehood altogether? Why should God promulgate a spe-cial precept forbidding lies, if every man was to be free to give to the precept itself two opposite interpretations—that is, to understand it either as forbidding people to state what is false, or as commanding them never to state anything else except what is false.

But we may put the thing in a stronger light still.

The only reason why the Commandments are binding on the human conscience is because revelation teaches that they are the expression of God's will in regard to man. Apart from this revealed teaching, they can have no obligatory power at all. Take away the divine truth that there is one God, and one only—that He is the Creator, Sovereign Lord of all—that He is to be worshipped by His creatures, and the first Commandment is meaningless and without force. Put aside the doctrine that He is infinitely powerful, infinitely wise, infinitely good—that He is all pure and all holy—that His name is, therefore, to be hallowed, and the second Commandment ceases to bind. Cancel the revelation that our neighbor's soul is made to the divine image—that it is the divine will we should love him, and those Commandments that refer to the duties of fraternal charity lose all their binding force. It is the doctrines on which they are founded that give to the Commandments their hold upon the will of man, and their claim to his obedience. And hence the only reason why we have no authority to change the Commandment is because we have no authority to change the doctrinal truth on which it rests. And if we have no leave or privilege to take opposite views of God's revelation in one case, how can we have any leave or privilege to take opposite views of it in another?

Again, if God inscribed His Ten Commandments on tablets of stone, and had them preserved in the Ark that they might keep the form and meaning He originally gave them, and that He might show the high and important place that they occupied

Conclusion

in His divine mind, He surely intended there should be a means of preserving the doctrinal portion of His revelation in the sense and meaning it had at the outset.

If He deigned to reveal certain truths of faith, it was because He meant them to be heard and to be believed, and if He meant them to be heard and to be believed, it was undoubtedly because He set some value upon them. But in what sense could they be said to have any value in His eyes, if He merely cast them out upon the world and let men treat them as they liked, allowing them to be looked upon as meaning anything, or as meaning nothing, or as meaning two contradictory things in one and the same moment? With what show of reason can it be maintained that He attached any importance to them at all, if He intended that His people were to be at liberty to believe them or not to believe them, or to believe their opposites, or to believe anything else in their stead if they chose?

One of two things: either He never made a revelation at all, or, if He did, He cannot have left it to be the sport of men's whims and fancies. If He revealed certain doctrines to the world, it must have been with the intention that they should be not merely believed, but should be believed according to the meaning in which He revealed them. And the very same reason that would lead Him to reveal them would force Him to invent some means of making them always express the same sense, and of surrounding them with such guardianship as would render them secure against being tampered with by the ever-changing opinions, and idle, erring speculations of men.

When He took such care lest the precepts of the Decalogue should be changed, surely He must have taken quite as much care that the revelations made by His Divine Son should never be changed. And if that Divine Son Himself cleared and purged the Mosaic Law, which was to be made void, of the false traditions and interpretations of the Scribes and Pharisees, would He not take precautions lest similar false interpretations might be introduced in the course of time into the laws and doctrines that He Himself revealed for all ages? The revelations to which He referred in the words of the great commission were, to say the least, quite as important as those delivered to Moses on Mount Sinai. And doubtless those revelations of His New Dispensation, which He condescended to make to the world with His own lips, would have been committed to stone also, had He not designed to preserve their identity and sense by a guardianship still more sacred, of which we shall speak presently — that is, His own special help, His own special presence, His own personal supervision, nay, His own unerring voice ever speaking through His Church, which He meant to be His mouthpiece on earth throughout all time.

And now this opens out a new view of the matter before us — a view that, on the one hand, reveals clearly the hollow fallacies of indifferentism; and, on the other hand, brings out into striking prominence the irresistible claims of the Catholic Church to be the sole authorized, adequate, infallible guardian and teacher of all revealed truth.

The very fact that indifferentists disagree among themselves, not merely about things that they take the unwarrantable liberty of terming minor points of revelation, but disagree also as to what doctrines are to be regarded as the fundamental doctrines of Christianity — this, I may say, of itself is sufficient to establish two things: first, the unreasonableness and utter untenableness of their system, and, secondly, the necessity of an authoritative voice still speaking that can tell with certainty what has been revealed and what has not.

Conclusion

Let us dwell on this for a moment. The adherents of indifferentism differ even as to what are those truths that are to be deemed essentials, the peculiar doctrines, the vital doctrines, the leading idea, the great truth, of the gospel. Some say that it is the divinity of Christ, some the Redemption, some the Resurrection, some that divine charity is everything, and some that the immortality of the human soul is the essence of the gospel, and all that need be believed. They dispute over almost every doctrine that is spoken of as lying within the sphere of revelation. And hence their system, when taken to pieces, plainly means that God once, or at sundry times, revealed a number of doctrines with the design they should be believed, and that at the same time He left His people perfectly free to affirm or to deny every one of those truths from beginning to end, according as they thought proper. Is not this equivalent to saying that He made a revelation, and that it was utterly useless to make it, since men were quite as wise before it was made as after they received it?

But this is not all. The fact that indifferentists take opposite views about even the vital doctrines of Christianity is not only a refutation of their theory; it is at the same time proof sufficient; it compels us to the conclusion that if God ever vouchsafed to make a revelation to the world, He must have consigned it to such careful keeping as would preserve it always in its entirety and make it always express exactly the same thing.

Why should He reveal a doctrine unless He wished it to have always the same meaning? How could He wish it to have always the same meaning if He intended, when He revealed it, that men were to be at liberty to give it any interpretation they chose? And how could men at any time be certain of its true meaning unless there were to be from age to age an authoritative, definitive, infallible voice to tell its meaning? Unless there exist some such unerring authority on earth, there can never be any certainty about revealed doctrine of any kind, whether it be called fundamental or nonfundamental. Nay, there can never be any certainty even that those doctrines that are said to be revealed have been revealed at all.

And what is more, if that unerring voice spoke only during the first two or three, or four or five, or six or seven centuries, and then became silent and has never spoken since, how can there be any certainty now about those truths that ought to form the object of faith?

Unless it speaks still, even at the present moment, it is impossible to make an act of faith at all. For faith supposes certainty and excludes doubt: faith is incompatible with doubt, and undoubting faith I can never have, unless I regard as infallible the voice that teaches me what I am to believe.

Yet our Lord makes faith an essential condition of salvation; and the Apostle tells us that without faith it is impossible to please God (Heb. 11:6). Now, would God make faith a necessary qualification for entrance into heaven and then leave men in the impossibility of ever possessing it, of ever exercising it, of ever eliciting an act of it? In such a plight He must have left them, unless there is in the world some source of unquestionable authority that can tell for certain what has been revealed, how much has been revealed, what its true meaning is, and in what sense it is to be received.

Cardinal Manning, in his book *The Temporal Mission of the Holy Ghost* refers to this point:

> There are some who appeal from the voice of the living Church to antiquity, professing to believe that while the Church was united it was infallible, that then when

it became divided it ceased to speak infallibly, and that the only certain rule of faith is to believe that which the Church held and taught while yet it was united, and therefore infallible. Such reasoners fail to observe that since the supposed division, and cessation of the infallible voice, there remains no Divine certainty as to what was then infallibly taught.[74]

If it be urged that the Scriptures contain all the truths of revelation, the state of the case is not altered. The same reasoning holds good: for I answer, how can I be sure that the Scriptures, as they are now published, are identical with the Scriptures of the fourth and fifth centuries, unless an infallible authority tells me they are? How can I be sure they contain the Word of God at all, unless the same infallible authority tells me they do? How can I be sure whether the Catholic version or the Protestant is the correct one — the one that contains the truth, and nothing but the truth — unless I regard as infallible the decision of my informant?

If the authority that tells me that the Old and New Testaments are the Word of God is a fallible authority, and therefore a questionable one, then whether it is the voice of an individual or the voice of a hundred millions of individuals, I can have no certainty, and consequently cannot exercise faith. For the opinions of a fallible multitude, equal in number to the whole population of the earth, as long as there is question of the things that are beyond the reach of reason, can never produce certainty of any kind, much less absolute, infallible certainty.

---

[74] Henry Edward Manning, *The Temporal Mission of the Holy Ghost: Or, Reason and Revelation* (New York: Appleton, 1866), 86.

But granting that the Scriptures contain the whole truth and nothing but the truth, and putting aside the question of which version is the right one, let us test the matter on another ground. How can I be sure which is the true interpretation of those passages from which are drawn contradictory doctrines with regard to points that are commonly called points of fundamental importance—such as the passages that refer to the Eucharistic presence and sacramental Confession—unless I have an infallible teacher to guide, enlighten, and instruct me?

I think, then, we are warranted in drawing the conclusion, that if God ever came into the world for the purpose of making a revelation and of instituting a Church, He must have established an unerring interpreter of the one and an unfailing ruler of the other, since there was exactly the same reason for instituting a means of protecting the revelation against false meanings as there was for making the revelation at all.

To have acted otherwise would have been to defeat His own ends; for either He intended His revealed doctrines to have contradictory meanings, or He did not. If He did, then He changes, and He is the God of truth today and the God of lies tomorrow; or He is the God of truth and of lies in one and the same moment, for the same individual, and under the very same circumstances. If He did not intend them to have contradictory meanings, then He cannot have abandoned them to every chance interpretation and to every human caprice. He must have raised up around them ramparts of defense that would protect them against the encroachment of innovation, and prevent their being wrecked by the ever-varying judgments and wandering imaginations of men.

Yes, being the unchanged, unchanging, and unchangeable God, the same yesterday, today, and forever (Heb. 13:8), He must have established on earth an undying authority, whose infallible

Conclusion

voice would speak in His name throughout all the vicissitudes of time and throughout the coming and passing away of all generations down to the day of doom—an authority whose voice would proclaim to the world, with unerring certainty, those doctrines that He revealed, and those only, and declare to all men the sense in which they were to be understood.

Either this must be granted, or a system of faith there cannot be, since otherwise absolute certainty about the object of faith there cannot be. Well then, dear reader, raise your eyes, look around you, inquire, examine.

Is there any Church on earth in which this unerring authority is found—in which this infallible voice speaks?

Where is it?

Which is it?

One and one only claims it. It is that one that alone can give sufficient reason for urging the claim—the one that, from her mark of everlasting, undivided unity, and from her inborn power of universal expansion, we have shown to be the one only true Church of the living God on this earth.

Bibliography

Aquinas, Thomas. *Truth.* Library of Living Catholic Thought. 3 vols. Chicago: H. Regnery, 1952.

Augustine. *Against the Fundamental Epistle of Manichaeus.*

———. *On True Religion.*

Bede. *The Ecclesiastical History of the English Nation.* Vol. 1. London: James Bohn, 1845.

Bèza, Théodore de. *Epistles.*

Browne, Edward Harold, and J. Williams. *An Exposition of the Thirty-Nine Articles, Historical and Doctrinal.* New York: H. B. Durand, 1865.

Calvin, Jean, and Jules Bonnet. *Letters of John Calvin.* Vol. 2. New York: B. Franklin, 1973.

Colledge, T. R., Esq., "Suggestions with Regard to Employing Medical Practitioners as Missionaries to China." *Chinese Repository* 9 (1836): 386–389.

Cyril of Jerusalem. *Catechetical Lectures.*

Epiphanius. *Panarion.*

Eusebius. *Ecclesiastical History.*

Irenaeus. *The Writings of Irenaeus.* Ante-Nicene Christian Library. 2 vols. Edinburgh: T. and T. Clark, 1868.

Macaulay, Thomas Babington. *Critical, Historical, and Miscellaneous Essays and Poems.* 3 vols. Philadelphia: Porter and Coates, 1879.

Manning, Henry Edward. *The Grounds of Faith: Four Lectures Delivered in St. George's Church, Southwark.* London: Burns and Lambert, 1852.

————. *The Temporal Mission of the Holy Ghost: Or, Reason and Revelation.* New York: Appleton, 1866.

Milman, Henry Hart. *History of Latin Christianity.* 9 vols. London: John Murray, 1867.

Mitchell, John. *The Life of Wallenstein, Duke of Friedland.* London: J. Fraser, 1840.

Moriarity, David. *A Letter on the Disendowment of the Established Church.* Dublin: John F. Fowler, 1867.

Newman, John Henry. *Certain Difficulties Felt by Anglicans in Catholic Teaching Considered.* 5th ed. London: Burns and Oates, 1879.

————. *Discussions and Arguments on Various Subjects.* 3rd ed. London: Pickering, 1878.

————. *Lectures on the Present Position of Catholics in England: Addressed to the Brothers of the Oratory.* 2nd ed. London: Burns and Lambert, 1851.

Pacianus. Epistle 1, *Ad Sympronian.*

Bibliography

Pope, Alexander. *The Works of Alexander Pope Esq.* Vol. 3, *Containing His Moral Essays*. Dublin: printed for George Faulkner Abraham Bradley, and Thomas Moore, 1751.

"Spiritual Destitution in the Metropolis." *London Quarterly Review* CIX (January–April 1861): 216–241.

Wiseman, Nicholas Patrick. *Lectures on the Principal Doctrines and Practices of the Catholic Church.* 3rd ed. London: Thomas Baker, 1888.

Sophia Institute

Sophia Institute is a nonprofit institution that seeks to nurture the spiritual, moral, and cultural life of souls and to spread the Gospel of Christ in conformity with the authentic teachings of the Roman Catholic Church.

Sophia Institute Press fulfills this mission by offering translations, reprints, and new publications that afford readers a rich source of the enduring wisdom of mankind.

Sophia Institute also operates two popular online Catholic resources: CrisisMagazine.com and CatholicExchange.com.

Crisis Magazine provides insightful cultural analysis that arms readers with the arguments necessary for navigating the ideological and theological minefields of the day. Catholic Exchange provides world news from a Catholic perspective as well as daily devotionals and articles that will help you to grow in holiness and live a life consistent with the teachings of the Church.

In 2013, Sophia Institute launched Sophia Institute for Teachers to renew and rebuild Catholic culture through service to Catholic education. With the goal of nurturing the spiritual, moral, and cultural life of souls, and an abiding respect for the role and work of teachers, we strive to provide materials and programs that are at once enlightening to the mind and ennobling to the heart; faithful and complete, as well as useful and practical.

Sophia Institute gratefully recognizes the Solidarity Association for preserving and encouraging the growth of our apostolate over the course of many years. Without their generous and timely support, this book would not be in your hands.

www.SophiaInstitute.com
www.CatholicExchange.com
www.CrisisMagazine.com
www.SophiaInstituteforTeachers.org

Sophia Institute Press® is a registered trademark of Sophia Institute.
Sophia Institute is a tax-exempt institution as defined by the
Internal Revenue Code, Section 501(c)(3). Tax I.D. 22-2548708.